MAGIC LADAKH

A VILLAGER OF NUBRA.

One of many who earn their summer living by transporting merchandise over the high passes on their yaks, ponies or dzos.

MAGIC LADAKH

AN INTIMATE PICTURE OF A LAND OF TOPSY-TURVY CUSTOMS & GREAT NATURAL BEAUTY

BY

"GANPAT"

(MAJOR M. L. A. GOMPERTZ
10th Baluch Regiment, Indian Army)

Author of "The Road to Lamaland" "Harilek'
"The Voice of Dashin" &c. &c.

With Illustrations & Map

London

Seeley, Service & Co. Limited

196 Shaftesbury Avenue

1928

"'Ganpat' was the sobriquet the sepoys had bestowed on the Captain when, as a very callow second lieutenant, he had been posted to an Indian infantry regiment. He was long and thin, and it would have been difficult to conceive anyone more unlike the conventional presentment of the jovial, pot-bellied, elephant-headed deity of good fortune known to India at large as 'Ganesh,' and to the Mahrattas as 'Ganpat.' But it was the nearest his men's tongues could get to his real name, and so it stuck."—"Landgrabbing," *Blackwood's Magazine*, 1916

The Nāgri inscription below the god's picture is his name; pronounced "Guṅput." He is a kindly soul, and even the mouse gets a meal in his shelter.

Printed in Great Britain
by The Riverside Press Limited
Edinburgh

CONTENTS

LIST OF ILLUSTRATIONS

CHAPTER ONE

THE ROAD FROM CIVILIZATION

CHAPTER ONE

The Road from Civilization

SOMEWHERE Kipling has a verse to the effect that to each and all of us was appointed some particular corner of the earth to be our own—some spot which should hold us more than any other. He wrote that verse about the county of Sussex, one of the most charming counties of a country notable throughout the world for its soft, garden-like beauty and its unfailing charm.

With the wonderful accuracy which generally characterizes his expression of human feelings he put into words an idea with which I think all, or nearly all, of us are in complete agreement. Only for some it is not the beautiful corners that appeal so much as the wilder or stonier bits of the world.

Take this great Empire of India alone, wherein I am writing, and which contains within its boundaries almost every type of terrain one can imagine, from the high-flung ice-peaks of the roof of the world—vast expanses of nothing but snow and ice and gaunt naked rock—through the dense tropical forest below the foothills, to the sandy wastes of desert, Rajputana and Kathiawar. India has the property of making people its own in some strange way, and to many of us it is our own country, for all that from almost every angle of view, by virtue of our race, we are utterly unakin to its inhabitants.

Yet to each and all of us who serve and love this immense country there is some special corner of it which calls as strongly as though we had been born and bred there, as though the roots of our being were set in its soil instead of being rooted for centuries in the little corner of Western Europe which is the nursery of British civilization and of the great nations and countries sprung from our blood and our traditions.

To one man it is the jungles and forests of Central India—teeming with wild life of all types—that call year in and year out. For another it is the arid rocks of the North West Frontier, that he hates and loves alternately, which hold him in thrall. To others still it is the sun-baked riverine earth of the Punjab plains, the smell of the cold-weather dawn in the fertile canal districts, the scent of wood smoke at dusk, the brazen sky of midday, the formless indigo and maroon of evening above the low haze, that are the picture of the land he would serve rather than any other. And to some again it is the High Snows that call, the waste places on the edge of Empire, the sparsely peopled patches among the great glaciers and the high peaks.

But why we are so made no one can tell us. The only solution that seems to answer the problem at all satisfactorily is one which is obviously out of count in this material modern age—namely, that which Kipling voices:

> "God gave to men all earth to love,
> But, since our hearts are small,
> Ordained to each one spot should prove
> Beloved over all."

That solution being out of court, since it predicates a personal Creator, there is another to fall back on—wildly improbable, but apparently to many folk much easier to believe than is the simplicity of the older one. It is that we are all reincarnated, that the life we lead at the moment is but one in an uncounted series of lives stretching back into the mists of the past—lost in the far fogs of the future. It is quite fashionable to believe this nowadays, more particularly, I think, in America.

So perhaps that is why to me, among others, the corner of the world that calls more hauntingly, more insistently, than any other is the High Snows of the Himalayan and trans-Himalayan ranges, which fling their giant barrier along the north of India. I must, doubtless, have been in one or more of my previous lives—probably in many of them—a Tibetan coolie, or possibly a pack-animal of the high passes; and therefore, whenever opportunity offers, I take the road into those simpler parts of the world where there are no railways and no motor-cars—no roads, indeed, by European standards

—only rough mule-paths or coolie-tracks, beaten and unbeaten trails over glaciers and snow-beds and along the beds of rivers, where the towering walls of the rock gorges dwarf into nothingness the slow, crawling caravans of donkeys, ponies, yaks and, sometimes, laden sheep.

To me the High Snows in general, and Ladakh in particular, exercise an attraction which is irresistible. Other people also find the same thing, and this year it was my fortune to be able to pass over six months wandering in Ladakh with a camera and a typewriter, seeking to make pictures in words or by plate or film of all I saw—the quaint types met by the roadside, the fascinating villages and monasteries, the women, the children, the red-clothed lamas, even the Skushoks, who are reincarnations of past Buddhas and so holy that they might escape rebirth for ever, but of their charity condescend to return in mortal guise to this sinful world to help its suffering inmates.

And that is the reason and excuse for this book. Once upon a time, not when we were very young, but when our great-grandfathers' ancestors were very young, a picture was sufficient in itself. In this vulgarized modern world it is necessary to gild the lily by adding quantities of letterpress to the pictures; and this I have tried to do.

If, reader, you, like me, love the quainter corners,

the quainter people of the world—even if, like me, you refuse to believe that this trait of ours is due to forgotten lives of our own—then in exchange for an hour or two of your time I will try to show you, as much as can be shown through the medium of mere words, one of the most fascinating countries I have ever seen—Ladakh, which I call Lamaland, and which was once the westernmost sub-kingdom of mysterious Tibet.

One has to get there, of course, and that is one excuse for travel books—they will take you in a few minutes to places which would otherwise require days and days of steamer or railway or car, and weeks and months of weary plodding on foot or little pony, ere you could reach them. I suspect the wizard in *The Arabian Nights* who invented the Magic Carpet had a family connexion with the publishing trade of the day—long-bearded, large-turbaned, spectacled old men, lovingly passing their days in the sunlight, copying old scrolls in flowing curves of Persian characters that were in themselves a picture.

Let us assume that we are already in India, for everybody, except the Europeans who live out here for years on end, knows all about India. The shipping companies and the Indian railways grow rich on the fares received from the erudite Members of Parliament, globe-trotters, and world's workers generally, who come out here for a few weeks' holiday preparatory to writing masterly treatises on the question of India. At the end of a month they can deal with the subject exhaustively and with complete finality. I, having been out here for only some twenty-odd years, know very little about India, but have enough self-confidence to feel that if I were allowed to spend another fifty years here, or to pass half-a-dozen of my potential future lives here, I would begin to realize some little of the fringes of the subject that I had yet to master.

Let us assume ourselves therefore in India, and to shorten our journey let us imagine that we have arrived in Rawal Pindi, where we have left the train and piled ourselves into a motor-car, with its bonnet pointed up the Kashmir road, and a two-hundred-mile motor-drive ahead of us—rather less than two days' journey along the Jhelum Valley road—now hung above the rushing torrent on a cliff-cut road, now crossing some small expanse of level fields hidden in the great mountain folds, emerging at last from the Baramula gorge into the ever-widening valley of Kashmir.

Let us thank books again, and, transporting ourselves at once to the end of the weary two hundred miles, enter into Srinagar, capital of Kashmir, a city built upon the waters of the Jhelum, ringed with beautiful lakes, adorned with the dream-gardens of the great Mogul emperors, to whose rule we British succeeded; like them, aliens also to India, and like them, therefore, naturally fitted to govern a country whose hallmark is myriad diversity—diversity of terrain, of peoples, of customs, of tongues, of creeds.

We might spend a minute or two in Kashmir looking round. It is the greenest, most fertile land we are likely to see for a long time, and to me it is Arcadia, this wide valley ringed with its forested hills, climbing ever till they merge into the almost unbroken ring of snow-clad peaks that, like a girdle of ivory, encircle this most beautiful of Eastern lands.

One gazes at Kashmir, with its marvellous colouring of snow and tree and lake: turquoise of slow-moving water under green and silver-green of fir and pine, poplar and great chenar tree, flower-strewn meadows and flower-spangled lawns; soft colouring of old Mogul brickwork, and gleam of hewn and carven stone softened by the passage of centuries; soft cloud-dappled sky over rich fields of grain and far vistas of snow, that at dawn and evening hold all the roses and pinks and madders of the palette. And as one looks one understands why it has always held such charm for India's conquerors—for the rough fighting men who, through the ages, have swept in over the passes; gaunt, gruff-voiced men, to whom the sword-hilt was familiar from childhood, the pen unknown even in grey old age; men—real men.

There is an old instinct in human nature that

beauty is good, that women should be beautiful so that they may reward men after toil and battle. This idea is, I know, looked upon as archaic by many people —archaic and evil—but human nature still believes it even if it does not dare to say so. That we do believe it is obvious from the vast outcry during the late war anent the decay of morals—to wit, the desire of women in large numbers to reward the men who had faced death, and, with their beauty, to give joy to those who might so soon die.

Perhaps it is the same also with countries—that there are male countries and female ones, and some of these last are beautiful as women. Kashmir is of its essence feminine and of a surety beautiful—beautiful, above all, to the men who had fought their way in over the passes through the naked savage hills of the north-west.

And, as so often happens in such countries, its women draw something from the land—they also have beauty. And, as often happens again, in such cases the men are hardly men. The most accurate description yet penned of the Kashmiri is that of E. F. Knight in *Where Three Empires Meet*: "That bearded athletic-looking disgrace to the human race."

Utterly devoid of courage in any form, moral or physical, the Kashmiri man, as a rule, possesses the whole gamut of mean qualities that go with such a lack of man's first attribute. I once watched a Kashmiri quarrel between two boatmen—the river-boat life is a feature of Kashmir. The quarrel was sustained and bitter, and supporters flocked to each side. Streams of high-pitched invective were poured forth, doubtless, in true Oriental fashion, concerned chiefly with the morals, or rather lack of morals, of the quarrellers' womenkind, much of it more probably true in Kashmir than elsewhere in the East. But, unlike most of these quarrels, this had an abrupt finale. Stung beyond bearing by the insults, one man at last seized the loose end of a cloth and with it deliberately flicked his opponent upon the shoulder. Amid a dead silence the gathering broke up, shudderingly and furtively fleeing away to their boats, aghast at the spectacle of one man raising his hand against another.

Not unnaturally, therefore, the Kashmiri does not rule himself. He has had many dynasties of rulers in the past, and the latest comers are the Dogras of Jammu—excellent fighting men and distinctly strong-handed rulers. In addition to holding Kashmir they hold also the territories beyond, Baltistan and Ladakh, and are suzerains of Gilgit and Hunza Nagar, and thus the Ruler of Jammu holds the northern border of the Indian Empire.

Srinagar is also, in a way, the terminal of the Central Asian trade: at least, it is the point where the change is made from pack-animal to motor-transport, and in the Yarkandi serai you may see a mixed crowd of Yarkandis from Chinese Turkestan, Ladakhis and true Tibetans, merchants and pilgrims bound for Mecca, resting after their eight-hundred-mile march over the passes before taking the two-hundred-mile car journey down to Rawal Pindi, where they will board the train—most of them for the first time in their lives—on the way to the ports, whence run the steamers to the Red Sea.

To these, also, Kashmir—with its pine forests, its rivers, the great expanse of the Dal Lake, with its quaint floating gardens borne on the surface of the placid waters, gardens built up of the roots of the water-weeds kept in position by long stakes driven into the lake-bed—must seem a veritable paradise after the arid countries they have left, where almost the only trees to be seen are the willows and poplars planted by the hand of man around the little scattered villages.

But the people of Central Asia are essentially travellers of the real type. They take the road for weeks and months together—men, women, and even little children—mile after mile, perched high on the stocky little ponies, riding upon their heaped bundles of bedding, merchandise and household gear, sitting like sacks upon a heap of sacks, as the slow-footed animals follow the age-old tracks, lined in the bad places with the whitened bones of those who have fallen by the wayside.

And thus we shall find them in the Sind Valley as we set out on the earlier marches of our journey to Ladakh, having covered the first stage from Srinagar to Gandarbal in one of the country boats, sometimes poled, sometimes paddled, sometimes towed, and so come at evening to the mouth of the fertile Sind, where its hurrying snow-fed waters widen out into a more slowly flowing stream, bearing now on its surface the clumsy picturesque craft of the Kashmir river—heavily built barges piled high with grass, or forming the living-quarters of a family or two: aged grey-haired grandmother, mothers with babies at breast, joyously dirty but happy children, a cow or two, a few goats and some clucking fowls.

We shall find these pilgrims of the road in fur-edged caps, with shapeless quilted garments, felt leg wrappings and long leather boots, as from Gandarbal we march to Kangan, amid its walnut-trees—its terraced fields and little wooden houses reminiscent of old pictures of the English countryside—our baggage clattering after us on the backs of a dozen Sind Valley ponies, whose ancestors from the dawn of history have carried the merchants' and travellers' goods up and down the Central Asian road on which we have now set our feet.

Kangan to Gund next day, twice crossing the silver

waters of the Sind river, the valley more and more fertile, with its grainfields and fruit-trees, and on either hand the great blue-green hills sweeping up to the snow peaks, soft, friendly hills, heavily clothed in pine and fir, and rich with wild flowers.

Then from Gund we pass to the long gorge of Gaggangir, which for years to come should prove a barrier to any form of wheeled transport, where the river is hemmed in between immense limestone cliffs, and our road is a rough mule-track, up and down, up and down, here high above the hurrying waters in the shadows of the firs, there dropping low to snake its way across long snow-slides, last remnants of the winter avalanches.

And on the road always the same travellers: the laden, unhurrying pack-animals; sandal-wearing, shouting, bearded Kashmiris; dark, stocky, slant-eyed men from Dras, with shapeless leather *pubbos* on their feet and tinder pouches at their belts; black-coated, long-booted traders from Turkestan on high Yarkandi ponies; loose-gowned pig-tailed Tibetans of Ladakh, with their string-woven shoes, their almost hairless faces framed in the fur flaps of the caps—a joyously laughing, stout-hearted people, for all that the only use they know of for water is drinking.

Then to Sonamarg, with its long meadows and its glacier valley—Sonamarg lying between 8500 and

9000 ft., with all the clarity of air that belongs to the fringe of the high places—Sonamarg framed in hills again, rolling slopes of wooded hills or gaunt, serrated walls of limestone sharp cut against the cloudless blue sky.

And so on again to Baltal, among the birch groves, under the high ramparts of limestone framing the Zoji La Pass, over which next day we shall make our way out of Kashmir, and from near the summit look our last upon the rich wooded beauty of the Sind Valley, with its wealth of water flowing down to the fertile fields we left a few days back.

And, since snow is late and heavy on the pass, we shall have to be under way very early—perhaps at midnight, when snow is hard and frozen and the avalanches are less to be dreaded, the avalanches that make the Zoji such a place of ill omen in the spring months, for all that its height is only some 11,500 ft.—a pygmy among the passes we shall meet later, and not so much a pass as a step of a giant's stairway, since on the farther side we shall hardly drop at all.

But, when daylight finds us over the pass, following the snowfields towards the bleak, huddled buildings of Macchoi, we know we are in a new country, that Kashmir has been left behind. The trees are gone, the hills are hard and savage-looking, and we know that all the sweetness and the softness of Nature has deserted us. We have come into a new world of hard rock and stone, of immense distances and of great heights, a land where the sun scorches by day and the water chills into ice at night, where life is hard and luxury unknown, and where Nature's moods are quite other than those she shows to us in the softer lands we have left.

And when we march onward day after day over the stony tracks above the rushing torrents, with hardly ever a tree to shade us, and where more often than not the discovery of a village marks the end of the long day's march, we understand better something of the charm of all we have left. And yet, all the same, there is a fascination in this new gauntness, a fascination more apparent perhaps to us civilized people than to others. One feels somehow that one has been stripped of much that hampers vision, one is alone with nature—naked in front of life—and one understands oneself the better for it, now that the conventions of life have gone, that the veils and curtains have been drawn aside and we have been set down in immensity to see ourselves as the giant hills must see us—if their vision is microscopic enough to see us at all—infinitesimal dots in an immensity of space.

And yet these countries seem not to breed at all the atmosphere of atheism that is produced so continuously by the overcrowded ant-heaps of civilization. One realizes, if one thinks at all, and most of us do in places like these, that there is something behind it all —that it is the creation of an artist and, still more, that the artist spark is alive in each and all of us, to fan or let die as we will. It is the infinitesimal dot that counts more than the giant hills.

So, as at last one slips down into Kargil, which is almost the very edge of Buddhist Ladakh—hitherto our way has lain through Purigh, which is part of Baltistan, and whose mixed peoples of partly Dard and partly Mongol stock are Mussulman by faith—one feels that the man who wrote, "God made the mountains and then made man to climb them," had probably more knowledge of the real truth of things than any of the sparkling self-sufficient intellects who succeeded him.

Ladakh is filled with a hotchpotch of peoples—Mussulmans who are Mussulmans; Mussulmans who are three-quarter Buddhists; Buddhists who are really Animists or devil-worshippers. But everybody believes in something, and it seems to me, after a good many months, that even the civilized people who come here believe also.

Be that as it may, it is a country of dreams and visions, and a country that seems to show you yourself in a wonderful way, which is perhaps why the unbelieving do not come here—mirrors are repulsive to some folk —and when one drops down into Kargil, and so on to the fringe of Ladakh, and sees for the first time the real Tibetan Buddhist in the bazaar, and one changes one's dull, weedy, *dras* ponymen for laughing, chaffing Ladakhis, one feels—at least I do—that one has come into something familiar and attractive, that one's feet are somehow on the road to home, for all that the road leads on into the unknown.

CHAPTER
TWO

THE COUNTRY

CHAPTER TWO

The Country

A DOZEN or so miles from Kargil lies the boundary of Ladakh proper. Although it is the administrative boundary and also the religious boundary—since across it we shall find Buddhists, whereas Purigh, of which Kargil is the capital, is Mussulman—yet in no other way does the country greatly differ from Baltistan, save that the general altitude is higher.

Ladakh is a country of true Tibetan type, which is a good way of expressing the difference between these countries and those to southward. Their chief characteristics are the extremely small rainfall and the great altitude above sea-level. The monsoon rains, which are swept up from the Indian Ocean and the Bay of Bengal, are finally halted at the wall of the Himalayas, and only stragglers of clouds find their way across into the countries beyond.

The first most noticeable result is that, while the south side of the Zoji La—the Sind Valley—is thickly forested, to northward at much the same altitude there are to all intents and purposes no trees at all. The grassy pine- and fir-clad slopes give place suddenly to gaunt hillsides of naked rock and disintegrating stone, scorched with the intense heat of the midday sun, frozen by the great fall of temperature which is such a marked feature of night in all arid countries, so that the rock and stone literally crumble away under the process.

From Kainpathri, at the head of the Zoji, where we left the last straggling glades of silver birch, gnarled and twisted by their efforts to make head against the snow, we stepped suddenly into a country void of any veil of trees. As a consequence, the variations of temperature become more and more marked, so that in the Ladakh winter you may at times sit in the sun and wonder which will be your first calamity—sunstroke on the sunny side of your body or frost-bite on the shady one. Trees somehow ensure a more equable temperature, with far fewer variations.

Even before you reach Kargil—in the stages from the Zoji to Dras and on down the Dras and Shingo Shigar rivers, till you come at last to the fertile strip of the Suru Valley near Kargil—you are struck by the lifelessness of the immense hills towering above you, where almost the only signs of life are little red-throated lizards and, rarely, a covey of *chikor*—the big partridge of the Indian frontier hills.

And yet these great limestone mountains are but dwarfs to what you will see later, though their average elevation surpasses that of the Alps, and the camping-places where you have sought shelter from the driving winds, and which seemed really high—eight and nine and ten thousand feet above the far-distant sea—are at low altitudes compared with those you will find later on in the journey.

Somebody once described Ladakh as being, if not the "Roof of the World"—a term generally applied to the Pamirs—as "at least the Attics." But I think more correctly Ladakh could lay better claim to being the actual roof. This little, forgotten country, some two hundred miles broad from south to north, by about three hundred long from east to west, contains a great portion of what is the biggest *massif* of mountains in the world—the Karakorum. The Karakorum range for practical purposes forms the northern boundary of Ladakh, although actually the undemarcated boundary between Ladakh and Chinese Turkestan runs well to northward; but since there are no inhabitants, and no villages for several hundred miles, nobody has ever worried their heads much about the actual frontier of these parts.

And the Karakorum range is truly real mountains. A glance along the peak-line will show you that, since you commence with K2, the second-highest mountain in the world, 28,250 ft., pass through Broad Peak, over 27,000 ft., the Gasherbrums at 26,000 odd ft., Teram

Kangri, with its 24,000 foot peaks, and then turn south-eastward into the line of the Shyok Nubra peaks of 24,000 and 25,000 ft. And between these lie literally scores of nameless giants, between 21,000 and 23,000 ft. —one great wilderness of ice-and-snow-clad mountains, at whose feet wind immense glaciers through a country utterly uninhabited, and where the only signs of human life are to be found in the rare traces of fire-blackened stones or circular shelters of boulders put up by some long-forgotten caravan. Memories and traditions of routes there are many—of fugitive kings, of venturesome merchants who have sought new ways across the ice world and vanished from human ken. Once, and I think once only, has a human skeleton been found—by the Mason Expedition this year—a man who had apparently fled into the mountains, lost his way and died there, with his little bundle of ragged clothing, a few pots of cheap German dye, and a rupee bearing the date 1921.

The passes through the range lie between 17,000 and 18,000 ft., and their crossing at the spring opening is in itself a feat of honest mountaineering, when their glaciers and moraines alike are hidden in one unbroken blanket of white snows, and the little stone cairns and the long line of pony skeletons, which normally point your road, are alike hidden from view.

Southward of the Karakorum, and separated from

A TYPICAL LADAKH GORGE.
The road passes through the Lamayuru defile.

it by the Shyok river, which is born in the thirty-mile Remo glacier on the east side of the Shyok Nubra divide, and which some hundred miles from its source is augmented by the Nubra river, child of the greatest glacier in the world outside the Polar regions—the Siachen, forty-seven miles long—lies the Ladakh range, a lower range, whose average height is only some 3500 ft. more than that of Mont Blanc, though here and there the peaks rise a couple of thousand feet higher.

South of that again lies the Zanskar range, cut off from the main chain of the Ladakh range by the great Indus river, in whose comparatively fertile valley lies the Leh country, the centre of old Ladakh. The Ladakh portion of the Zanskar range is about the same height as the Ladakh range, though to southward it runs higher again, up to the 22,000 and 23,000 ft. of the Suru peaks, which are not truly in Ladakh, though the country is Buddhist and the people of Tibetan stock.

From Kargil to Khalatse, where you emerge from the Lamayuru gorge into the Indus Valley, the country is all one tangle of slightly lower peaks and mountain masses.

Thus, looking at the country from south to north, we see three great mountain chains containing two great valleys—the Indus and the Shyok—the true floor of Ladakh, and on the meridian of Leh, which is more or less the centre of the country, the height of this floor is 11,000 ft. in the Indus Valley and 10,500 ft. in the

Shyok Valley. Westward, since both rivers flow westward, the valleys shelve slowly downward until the two rivers meet in Baltistan and the united waters cut their way through the Ladakh range into Gilgit territory, where they run at the low altitude of about 4000 ft. Eastward the country shelves upward into the Tibetan plateaux, and the floor of Ladakh in the eastern corner is over 14,000 ft. high.

Man is the most adaptable of all animals: he can live in the Polar regions and thrive in the tropics; he can flourish at sea-level, and he can keep alive at heights where the last animal life disappears. But nevertheless there are limits set upon his range with regard to altitude—limits, that is, as regards the range wherein he can live continuously year in and year out, and from generation to generation. And, broadly speaking, that limit seems to be in the vicinity of 15,000 ft. One might, in fact, say that somewhat below the summit of Mont Blanc gives the height-level at which man can live continuously, cultivate a few scattered fields, and build himself some form of permanent home.

He goes higher for the summer—the nomad peoples of Eastern Ladakh take their flocks and herds to 16,000 and even 17,000 ft. in summer, but winter drives them down again to the less rigorous altitudes of Shushal and the Pang Kong and Chang Tạng villages, mostly about 14,000 ft. Here there are real little houses of mud and stone—wood is almost non-existent and very valuable, so that the main form of fuel is yak dung—and fields of a sort where barley will ripen in the short summer.

Naturally, therefore, the greater part of inhabited Ladakh is the big river valleys—the Shyok, the Indus and the Nubra. These three are the chief centres of population, and villages are numerous, often not more than five or six miles apart, with quite big ones every now and then.

Always, however, one sees the same characteristics of country: great mountains—to eastward more of the rolling-hill type, to north and westward, gaunt, jagged peaks and saw-backed ridges—and everywhere, sometimes in full view, sometimes hidden in curved valleys, the glaciers, whence come down the waters which are the life-blood of Ladakh and the surrounding countries. Irrigation is the solution of Ladakh's problems; wherever water can be led down in the little carefully built and carefully maintained channels there are fertile fields and often artificially planted trees—little oases of green among the barren red and brown and chocolate hills—orchards of fruit-trees in the lower parts of the Shyok and Indus, apricot and apple, mulberry and walnut.

At some comparatively recent period of the earth's history Ladakh was under the sea. Later on, when it emerged, it was covered with an ice-cap sweeping right down from the North Polar regions. That ice-cap has been melting more or less continuously ever since, during the 100,000, 200,000, 300,000, or whatever number of years the latest geological text-books favour as the time that has elapsed since the world's most recent freezing.

But in Ladakh you cannot only see the traces of the ice's work at every turn, you can, moreover, see the remains of the actual ice-cap in many places, and so, if you have the gift of imagination, project yourself into the far-distant past, when man—in this part of the world anyway—was unthought of and unknown.

In the Karakorum, and in the mountains to eastward, you find rounded hills still covered with perpetual ice, ice-covered slopes that cannot be called true glaciers, since they have no snow-feeding basins such as glaciers require for their formation and continued existence. They are the remains of the original ice-cap which once formed an almost unbroken sheet from the Pole down to at least as far as Kashmir, which is, approximately, at the latitude of Southern Spain.

The ice is steadily melting away year by year, century by century, but meanwhile it is serving a purpose in providing irrigation water. Some day it will all have gone and then the Ladakhi will be faced by the problem which has already faced the people of Turkestan. There to northward lie the great Central Asian deserts of the

Gobi and the Takla Makan. They are dead with a deadness that perhaps exists nowhere else on earth—waterless wastes of sand that was once soil.

But in these wastes are to be found the remains of old towns, of old civilizations, paintings and writings in scripts whose very names are unknown. And since the dryness of the air is so intense, there also are the people to be found in their sand-buried graves just as they were laid to rest fifteen hundred or two thousand years ago. I have before me as I write a photo by Sir Aurel Stein showing the body of a man of Turfan buried fifteen centuries ago, and it is hard to believe that he is even dead.

And the reason Sir Aurel suggests for this desiccation of Central Asia is, that not so much has the climate changed, as that in the past those areas subsisted in the main on the excess water given by the slow melting of the original ice-cap, since the actual snowfall must have been insufficient to produce glaciers of a size to give the requisite summer volume of water. And so also it seems to me that that is to some extent the condition of Ladakh, and that at some not very distant time big areas of Ladakh also will gradually desiccate and cease to support human life.

But not for some time yet, for the snow and ice reservoirs of the mountain chains, notably of the Karakorum, are still immense, and much of it is wasted in summer, when the rivers flood down towards India, and so bring life and wealth to the Northern Punjab and to Sind, where recent researches have laid bare relics of civilization older than anything hitherto dreamed of in India.

The volume of water derived by the Ladakh glaciers is still vast, and from time to time it causes catastrophes, when the drainage is blocked and the slowly melting waters form great lakes behind their glacier barriers, and then finally, perhaps after many years, break their dams and pour down in floods, carrying all before them. This very year the Kumdan glacier in the upper Shyok river broke with the weight of water confined behind it, and the Shyok suddenly came down in flood in late October, a month when the great river is normally near its lowest and fordable in many places.

I took a keen interest in the news of that flood, for only a sudden change in my plans had prevented my being in the gorge of the upper Shyok in the latter part of October, and I do not think that anyone caught there by that flood would have come out again. Although I have not yet heard details, the flood must have been on a large scale, since it swept away the great suspension bridge at Tirit over the middle Shyok, which is nearly a hundred miles from the Kumdan glaciers.

As I said in the first chapter, the excuse for this book is supposed to be the necessity in a modern world of attaching letterpress to pictures. But I suppose it is really necessary to have just some idea of the country with which the pictures deal before one looks at them, especially if they happen to deal with a portion of the world a little off the beaten track, such as Ladakh happens to be.

And that is why, when we halted at Kargil at the end of the last chapter, I thought we might as well have a glimpse at the country we are about to enter, and I have tried to give a rough word-picture of what it will be like.

You are to imagine a triple series of great mountains enclosing big river valleys—sometimes several miles broad, filled with fields and little villages; sometimes narrow gorges, several thousand feet deep, holding nothing but the rushing waters of the summer floods or the low frozen stream of winter—and the narrow ribbon of the cliff-hung pony-track, passing at long intervals rough cantilever bridges of poplar trunks.

Farther east you will emerge from the tangled maze of mountains into more open country, where the 19,000 and 20,000 ft. mountains are more like rolling hills, with summits only 4000 or 5000 ft. above you—wide expanses of tussocky grass dotted with the black herds of yaks and here and there with the black tents of the nomads.

Northward from the comparatively fertile mouth of

the Nubra Valley you will follow the Central Asian trade route and, climbing away from human habitations, pass over the glaciers of the high passes under the giant peaks, here 7000 and 8000 ft. above you, for all that you yourself are well up between 17,000 and 18,000 ft., watching your yaks plunging through the snowdrifts or helping the breathless men dragging the panting ponies out of the soft places or man-handling the loads over the steep ice-slopes.

And in front of you will then lie the long line of the Aghil ranges on whose farther side the caravans descend slowly to the low level of Kashgaria or Chinese Turkestan —the true heart of Asia.

To westward, should you choose to follow down the Shyok river, lie Baltistan, Chitral, and Hunza Nagar, and so through the wild tribal country into the northernmost part of tourist India—Peshawar and the Khyber Pass, with its railway and its motor-cars, its cinema operators and newspaper correspondents, its picturesque tribesmen, so beloved of the globe-trotting photographer.

But I think you will find that Ladakh will give you things just as picturesque and just as attractive and, in addition, throw over you a charm that is all its own—a charm, a magic, that I have found in no other land.

So let us start the ponies again and take the road forward from Kargil towards our next stage, Moulbekh, where we shall really enter Lamaland and look upon

Two Ladakhi Ladies of Rank.

The head-dress (*peragh*) represents a snake of turquoise with coral tail. Ladies of rank wear shawls instead of the common goat skin cape.

Buddhists and *chortens* and *manes* and *gompas*, and feast our mortal eyes upon immortal Skushoks.

It is a long day's march from Kargil to Moulbekh, and much of it is typical Ladakh—bare and stony gorges, and steep places where the line of sight from your eye past your stirrup-iron comes to rest vertically below in the torrent-bed at a distance that makes you think of the problems you used to do at school about the properties of "g" and the pace at which a free falling body will hit the floor. So far as I remember, there was a catch, in that the problematic body was supposed to be in a vacuum, and although you may find that the Ladakh air is thin and unsatisfying until your red corpuscles have doubled themselves, you will still not be in a vacuum, and so will not hit the floor quite so fast as that problematic falling body. But you will hit it quite fast enough, so you had better give up thinking about it and trust your pony to get along. And do not worry about his habit of walking always on the outside of the ledge—you cannot get over inherited instincts, and for hundreds of years that pony's ancestors have chosen the outside of the ledge in order to avoid scraping their loads against the inner wall of the cliff and so being pushed off into space.

But in time we shall get out of the gorge and come to Shergol, and you will look upon your first *gompa*, which we of the West would call a monastery. It is pink and white and, apparently, plastered on to the face of an immense rock, but it has been there a long time and has not fallen down yet, so it will doubtless last for several more reincarnations of its lamas. Around you are white structures, from little pillars of a couple of feet to big ones ten and twelve feet high, and beyond those again lie walls, apparently meaningless, and covered with stone carved in unfamiliar writing. *Chortens*, these first, "bone places," in which are deposited the ashes of the mortal covering of the Buddhist; ashes moulded into little porkpie-like shapes. The walls are not meaningless either, for they are breastworks against devils, and you must leave them on your right hand, which is the same way as you pass wine in Europe. Then and then only will the carven stones bring you protection and good luck, and the mystic verse, "*Om mane padme hum*," from which the walls get their name of "Manes," bring credit to you in your rebirth into this or other worlds.

Then at last we shall camp at evening on a pleasant expanse of coarse grass under the shadow of a steep hill, crowned with a high-perched *gompa*, and perhaps watch other wayfarers pitching their evening camp in the shadow of a willow plantation: pig-tailed men, squatting in the shadows of the loads their patient ponies and half-bred yaks have carried all day, and preparing the inevitable buttered tea in the copper pots and the long black wooden churns which are slung upon their backs.

And then, as the sun goes down, and you look out over the valley, with its fantastic cliffs, wind- and weather-carved into hundreds of strange shapes—forts and towers and palaces—you will think that the Ladakhi is not so unreasonable in his beliefs after all, that Ladakh is a country where anything might be true, and where magic is properly at home. Only I think you will concede that it is good magic—white magic—and that the devils are only gnomes and elves.

Finally, when the sun is gone and the place is all shadows, lit only here and there by the wavering glow of the cooking fire, throwing up the silhouettes of the slant-eyed Mongolian-featured ponymen, and you listen to the low talk and the laughter, and see the buildings silhouetted against the sky, like pictures by Rackham, you will forget all that I have told you, or tried to tell you, about geography, and think only that you have come into a land of forgetfulness—a land where time is nothing—where facts matter not at all and only fancies have any value.

CHAPTER
THREE

THE PEOPLE

CHAPTER THREE

The People

IT is always a moot question as to whether the greater portion of the joy of travel lies in the seeing of new countries or in the meeting of strange peoples. Some folk will tell you that it is the first experience which is to them the more attractive—others again will say they prefer the second. I think probably that for the larger part of mankind it is the second which holds the greater charm, basing my opinion on the fact that it is always those photographs and pictures showing men and women of other lands that have a far stronger appeal than those which show only landscapes. In fact, it is quite a common thing to hear people remark how much more attractive a pictured landscape would be if it included some human figures.

I think also that most of us when travelling want not only to see the strange peoples, but to learn something about them—about their ways of life, their customs, their thoughts, their beliefs. A regret one so often hears expressed by travellers in out-of-the-way parts of the world is that of not being able to talk to the people in their own language, of being forced to converse through the entirely unsatisfactory medium of interpreters, these last often being people of entirely different race and creed, and with all the semi-educated person's narrowness of vision, unable to translate the thoughts of other races even if they happen to have the actual words at their command.

I, alas! do not speak Tibetan, which is the language of Ladakh, but I have been a little better placed than many travellers in that I do speak Urdu, with more than average fluency, and I had two really excellent Urdu-speaking Ladakhis with me, so that at least I got my knowledge from people of the country, even if it had to be passed through the medium of a tongue foreign to both sides.

The inhabitants of Ladakh are primarily Tibetans: race, history and religion alike combine to make them truly the same as the inhabitants of Greater Tibet, for all that for nearly a century they have been politically subject to the rulers of Kashmir. Where they differ is that, whereas Greater Tibet has been to a large extent a closed country to the outside world, Ladakh, lying as it does directly across the main trade route between India and Central Asia, has inevitably been an open country, interested to some extent in, and directly influenced by, her northern and southern neighbours.

Besides the Tibetans of true stock there are two other classes in the country: one is the mixed population, mostly to be found about Leh, the Arghuns, offspring

A Corner of a Picturesque Ladakhi Village on the Leh Road.

In the centre is a woman spinning by a prayer wheel.

of the unions between Ladakhi women and Kashmiri or Yarkandi fathers, Mussulmans all by virtue of their fathers; the other is Dards, a small survival of the Aryan races which at one time held Ladakh, before they were swamped by the waves of Tibetan incursions.

The Tibet type varies in the different districts: southward and westward it is less pure owing to admixture with the old Dard survivals; northward, in Nubra, it tends to show a certain Chinese stamp; eastward it is indistinguishable from the people of Tibet proper. Indeed, I was told that the nomad peoples of the Chang Tang country in the east are not Ladakhis at all, but Tibetans who remained there after the last invasion, which is a matter of recent history, when Western Tibet, or, as we now call it, Ladakh, had more or less separated from the greater country, but not as yet come under the hand of Jammu.

Actually, indeed, when an inhabitant of Ladakh speaks of a Ladakhi he means a man of the country around Leh—of the Indus Valley. A man from the east is a *Chang-pa*, someone quite different, while a *Nubra-pa* again is looked upon as being of a race distinct from the people of Ladakh proper.

The Tibetan tongue is of the Mongolian family, a syllabic and tonal language utterly unlike the European and Indian languages. It has also several dialects, which vary considerably, so that it is not at all easy for a man of Eastern Tibet to make himself understood by a Ladakhi, and vice versa. In Ladakh itself—speaking now of the country as it is politically constituted—there are differences even over distances of a couple of days' march, for the country is conservative and old speech and customs die hard, if they die at all.

Hundreds of years ago the Tibetan language was reduced to writing, in a form of script borrowed from India: one can recognize many of the letters of the Nagri alphabet, the old Sanskrit script used so largely in the modern Indian languages. The form of most of the letters has altered greatly now; but, even so, if one is told what sounds the characters represent it is easy to trace the resemblance between the two alphabets, and some letters are still unchanged.

But when the language was reduced to writing it was done once for all, and no subsequent allowance has ever been made for the change of word-form and of pronunciation which in Tibetan, as in every living language, has been going on ever since. The old gibe of the French schoolboy at English might well be hurled at Tibetan spelling: "You write it 'elastic' and you pronounce it 'indiarubber.'"

The Tibetan of Ladakh is, as one would expect from the altitude at which he lives, a man of comparatively small stature, though there are exceptions. The average height is probably not much above five-foot-four, and the women are considerably shorter. They are, as one also expects of people of the high countries, very sturdily built. I should think in the course of centuries they have actually developed chests and lungs relatively far bigger than ours to compensate for the rarity of the atmosphere.

The first impression they give you is one of swarthiness, but this is due mainly to dirt, for washing is not a common habit of either sex. But a well-washed Ladakhi baby, such as one may sometimes come across in the mission hospital, is quite fair, and I have seen many Ladakhis, both men and women, who would, I think, if they were subjected to a month's course of Turkish baths to get rid of the dirt of years, emerge considerably lighter in hue than the much-ablutioned Indian.

Their features are essentially Mongolian, high cheekbones and slanting eyes, and with very little facial hair, though sometimes one meets goat-bearded old men who make you wonder whether hairlessness is truly a Mongolian trait or merely the result of generations of hair-plucking with the little tweezers that men and women alike carry at their belts. The features of both Arghuns and Dards—the latter in particular—are Aryan, or nearly Aryan, in form, dependent upon the amount of Mongolian blood in their composition, and upon the myriad factors that govern the physical development of mixed races.

The three characteristics which I would select as most noticeable in the Ladakhi are cheerfulness, honesty and willingness to work. Courage perhaps also, not the courage of the fighting man so much as the courage of the sturdy animal. They will face hard work and exposure to height and cold, and go on laughing; they will march great distances carrying heavy loads, and live with very little in the way of food or comfort. Indeed, comfort, as we understand the term, is unknown to them—to rich or poor alike—even though the term "rich" in Ladakh would mean poverty in England and straitened resources even in agricultural India.

Of all the peoples I have met in the course of twenty years knocking about in the East I have never met one I found so easy to get on with, or whom I liked so much for so many traits, as the Tibetan of Ladakh. He would not make a soldier, of course; possibly the teachings of Buddhism have killed out the fighting spirit which at one time made the Mongol the dread of the civilized world. I do not think he will ever make a civilized human being as we understand the term. I think he will die in the process if anyone ever tries to civilize him. But as he is—and I for one would not wish to change him—a man of the wild high places; of the forgotten parts of the earth, it is hard to conceive anything more quaintly attractive. He always gives me the impression of a super-intelligent dog with a highly developed sense of humour.

There are all sorts of wonderful ways of studying man, judging by the endless books that appear yearly on the subject. You can take him, apparently, from all sorts of angles, and prove or disprove any particular theory you wish by marshalling hosts of tables about head measurements and hair formations. But what ordinary people like you and me really want to know is what the man or woman looks like, what they eat and wear, and what they believe, and what is their solution to the eternal problem of the relation between the sexes.

The Ladakhi Tibetan's contribution to this last problem is, like himself, peculiar, for he has adopted official polyandry, and the origin of the custom is lost in the dim ages.

The world has seen polyandry—the woman with two or more husbands—in many forms and in many ages and places, but it has been of sporadic occurrence. Nowhere else, I think, has there been an instance of a whole race adopting it and retaining it for countless centuries.

The eldest son of a Ladakhi family marries a wife either of his own volition, or else as arranged by the parents of both sides. The offer of his hand and fortune includes also the hand of his brother, or of two brothers next in age, but not their fortunes, since they have none. Any further brothers have to go out into a cold world and earn their own living.

The lady being duly married takes on both or all three brothers, and the children for all official purposes are the children of the eldest. But I believe, in respectable families, when the eldest brother is at home the others are expected to keep out of the way.

The question of polyandry is a thorny one, and all sorts of people write all manner of things about it, from theories proving that it is a natural law to keep down the increase of population in a barren country, to mere invective. The Mussulman, in particular, favours the last line of action. To him polyandry is most unutterably foul, whereas the reverse custom, polygamy, is the divine plan for the human race. To me personally this seems somewhat a case of the pot and the kettle.

One result, however, it does undoubtedly produce, and that is, a woman whose position is all that the most ardent feminist could desire. The Ladakhi lady is complete head of her own household, and the men are well underneath her extremely capable thumb. She has her own money; she trades on her own; her word is very much law. And, lastly, when she meets you on the roadside, she passes the time of day freely and cheerfully, which is most attractive to anyone who has spent long years in the veil-cursed East.

There is however another form of marriage, which I believe is also much practised in Europe and in America, though we do not invent a special name for it.

Suppose that there are no sons in a household. The property then descends to the daughter. She does not, as a rule, look out for an eligible trio of brothers. Instead she casts her eye round for a well-favoured younger son—one of those who, from being number three, four, or more, in his own family, has been thrust out to work in a cold and thankless world, and she marries him properly and legally with a lama to tie the knot, and thereafter he is known as her "Magpa." A magpa's lot is not a happy one; even the average English husband would probably rebel at it. He is in an entirely subordinate position, owns nothing, can do only what he is told, and, finally, can be thrown out without even the proverbial week's notice. I am told that many magpas after a few months would sell their souls—if they were their own—to get notice to quit.

Having sacked one magpa the lady may take another, and continue in the same way indefinitely. It is a good thing to be a woman in Ladakh, but it is even better to be an only child and a daughter.

The other noticeable result of polyandry is the paucity of children, with the consequent further result that poverty is unknown—I have never seen a beggar—and that no child is ever unwanted. Were a Ladakhi woman to abandon her infant—not that I can conceive such an event happening—there would be a score of families ready to snap it up. I believe, further, that an unmarried girl who has had a child is much sought for in marriage, since the birth of one child argues good prospects of her bearing others, and many marriages are sterile.

Ladakh is very much a self-supporting country, and produces everything, or nearly everything, it wants except tea, which is the staple drink of the country. Indeed, it is more than drink, since the Ladakhi, like the people of Tibet, makes his tea with butter, and it is more like strong rich soup than tea as we drink it. The tea comes from China via Tibet, and is boiled three times before use, so that it is a decoction and not an infusion. After the third boiling the cooking vessel, which then contains only a very little strong red liquid and the leaves, is filled to the brim again with hot water, allowed to simmer a little, the leaves strained off, and the contents emptied into a big wooden churn, into which butter is put, and the whole churned up with a little salt, and perhaps some soda added.

This and barley-meal are the Ladakhis' staple food, but those who can afford it eat meat as well in the evening. The barley is used in many forms, as puddings, cakes, and in a kind of shortbread which will keep good for a year or more. There are very few vegetables in

LADEN KASMIR COOLIES crossing a snow bridge over a mountain torrent.

THE MID-DAY MEAL, ON A HALT DAY, on the edge of the Chang Tang country. A Tankse man making and cooking sausages.

Ladakh, and the Ladakhi contrives to do without them, but those who can get them use large quantities of dried apricots, which grow in abundance in the lower valleys at places such as Nurla or Hundar.

Both the tea and the barley-meal are consumed from the little wooden bowls that all carry in the bosoms of their loose robes, the bowls often being lined with thin beaten silver, but the well-to-do prefer their tea in china handleless cups, on silver saucers, which are brought from China and Lhassa.

Last of all—which may or may not explain why Ladakh is such a popular country with globe-trotting citizens of the United States—there is *chang*, which is a fermented drink made of barley. The Ladakhi brews it and drinks it in large quantities, and contrives sometimes to get drunk upon it, which argues a perseverance that might be devoted to a better cause.

We have thus seen the three chief failings of the Ladakhi, which were succinctly expressed to me by an Indian: "He drinks wine; he doesn't wash, and one woman marries many men."

If I were a Ladakhi I should wash very little. An English upbringing is a difficult thing to break away from, and, as we all know, the first and greatest commandment of the law—even greater than that about the Sabbath day—is, "*Daily* shalt thou wash thy neck *and* behind thy ears." Even so, I recollect a period of ten days in Northern Ladakh when the only ablutions I performed were perfunctory washings of the finger-tips. One does not wash with a temperature at heaven knows how many degrees below freezing-point, and when your sole shelter is a tiny tent, wind-proof only because of the snow heaped up round it.

Also, were I a Ladakhi, I should consume much *chang* in the winter months, when there is no work possible to do, no amusements existing, and frost-bite a common fate to anybody rash enough to take the road. I should consume lots of it, and hope in time to get drunk and so forget the cold and dreariness. And as for polyandry—well, at least, it does not lead to all the nasty crimes that polygamy has produced in Oriental countries. Murder is still unknown in Ladakh and infanticide undreamed of. Jealousy does not seem to exist, and the horrid sense of "property," with which many married couples in more civilized lands seem to look upon each other, appears to be uncommon, except in the case of the poor magpa.

But I should be very grateful if some magic power would convert me into some being as cheerful as a Ladakhi can be when apparently there is nothing in the world for him to be cheerful about.

I do not think I could ever contrive to be gay if my sole worldly possessions were a pair of rather worn-out, home-made, string shoes; two ragged, home-woven, gown-like garments, worn one over the other for warmth; a greasy fur-edged cap to turn down over my face in a literally freezing gale; a wisp of hair off a yak's tail for snow-spectacles; a little bag containing a few handfuls of coarse-ground barley-flour and some tea-leaves and salt; perhaps an old tattered sheepskin coat to serve me as bed and tent; and I had a three-to-one chance of losing my ungloved fingers and my unsocked toes from frost-bite before I could get to the home—where big brother Bill will be sitting in lawful possession of my one-third of a wife as well as his own share.

If I could laugh honestly under those conditions I should consider myself what I call the Tibetan of Ladakh, well on the road to being a man, which is the best thing to be in all the world.

It sounds rather as if the Ladakhis looked utterly poverty-stricken, but they do not really because, like all more or less primitive people, they like bright colours and gaudy ornaments. As one would expect, they are mostly to be found on the women, and the Ladakhi woman, for all that her brown or red gown may be old and tattered, contrives to give a very vivid splash of colour to the landscape with the striking gaudiness of her head-wear.

Firstly she braids her hair into innumerable plaits, and then she fastens on to it two large flaps of black astrakhan, one on each side, which look like elephants' ears on a small scale. Between these she puts a long strip of scarlet cloth cut like a snake, with the expanded hood on top of her head, the head over her forehead, and the tail down her back. On this is sewn every turquoise she or her mother or grandmother—for it is an heirloom—have managed to buy or get, and finishes off the snake's tail with rows of coral beads. She may, if she has more money than most, intersperse the big turquoises with filigree gold ornaments sewn on to the red cloth.

Her ears bear bundles of silver earrings, and from the astrakhan ear-flaps droop gold or silver chains, while about her waist is a girdle, from which hangs an openwork brass or gold disc, as big as a saucer, suspending her household keys and manicure and toilet instruments. Her wrists are girt with large bracelets of shells—these from India mostly—and about her throat will be all the necklaces of gold or silver or corals or cheap beads she can afford. Lastly, if she be well-to-do, the usual goatskin cape will be replaced by a rich worked shawl of Bokhara.

The Chang Tang women of the East, in addition, finish off the *peragh*—the turquoise snake—with a bar of silver across their forehead, from which little metal pendants and silk tassels fall to the level of the eyes.

In fact, in spite of having three husbands, or else a

servile magpa, the Ladakhi woman likes to fulfil the universal law, which one hopes women will never seek to avoid, of trying to look attractive to the opposite sex. Even if you are a lady of much wealth, with a magpa husband, it is surely your business to make yourself attractive for him. When you see a Ladakhi lady whose face is smeared with fruit juice, and with the little pips of the fruit still adhering to her rather prominent cheek-bones, you must remember that she is swayed by exactly the same desirable sentiments as those which in women of a more civilized world bring large fortunes to the designers of lacy and frilly nothingnesses.

CHAPTER FOUR

BUDDHISM

CHAPTER FOUR

Buddhism

THE question which man, either individually or racially, has probably asked himself most frequently and most insistently ever since he became a thinking being—"Homo sapiens," as the scientists used to call him, to distinguish him from the other members of the animal creation to which physically he belongs—is the eternally recurrent one of the hereafter: "What happens to us when we die? What lies on the other side of this universal phenomenon of death?"

Through all the ages "Saints and Sages" have put forth their views, and sometimes man has accepted them and sometimes—the saddest case—he has rejected all of them and adopted the philosophy of Khayyám, the agnostic attitude:

> "But evermore
> Came out by the same Door as in I went."

One may, I think, in generalizing, ignore that small handful which hold, or say they hold, that death is finality, the complete end; that if anything remains it can be only some form of life-force which is absorbed into the totality of being, retaining no individuality, no intelligence, no volition.

Mankind as a whole, whether in a highly civilized or in a primitive state, clings firmly to the belief that death is not the end; that it may be a beginning of something better—as say the Christian and the Mohammedan; that it may be a passing to a similar existence elsewhere with the painful factors of the present life removed—the more common belief of primitive savages; or, that death is but the prelude to rebirth, in this or other worlds, either in a higher or a lower form.

This last view was the contribution of Hinduism, the old faith of India, and transmigration, as it is called, is the basic belief on which is built up the vast structure of Hinduism and Buddhism, the two allied religions which, so far as I can remember figures, number among their followers almost a third of the human race.

To us of the West—speaking again in general terms—this doctrine, with its lack of individuality, makes no appeal. Our individuality is something we feel too strongly—it is innate in the race; and whatsoever the Western man may think about his future, he is perfectly convinced that he is going to be himself and nothing else.

But to the Hindu thinkers the solution of the obvious injustices of life, as it is lived on the earth, must lie in a repetition of lives; the inequalities of one life must be balanced out in others; reward for virtue and punishment for vice must be reaped in lives yet to come—here, in the actual earth we know.

And, as an inevitable corollary, that scheme was held to cover not only man, but the whole living and sentient creation. And this, if you think of it, is only logical; for if, as is largely the case, man's most potent argument for further existence is the necessity of adjusting accounts, then the animal creation also requires it. The wild creature or the domesticated animal that has known only pain and misery must be compensated afterwards.

Personally, if ever I could get away from my firm conviction that man is something entirely different from the rest of the animal creation, whose form of body he shares, then I think I also should adopt this line of thought, since I cannot honestly reconcile myself to the idea that when my dogs die that is the end—that they have vanished from being for ever, that the sum of intelligence and devotion which makes up man's best companion is nothing but a chance combination of physical and chemical factors.

And, logically, what might be true of my dogs must equally be true of my sister-in-law's cat, or my ponies; and if you carry it on logically you will, as did the old Hindu sages, include everything, down to the smallest insect; and if they had possessed microscopes, which perhaps fortunately for them they did not, they would have had to drag in the various microbes as well.

Anyway they believed, and still believe, that man is merely the highest earthly stage of a long chain of spiritual evolution, and that the better you are in this life the better kind of man or woman will you have a chance of being in your next earthly life—with the chance, also if you have been very bad, of reverting to animal or insect existence, and so having all the long ladder to climb again.

But even so, what of the ultimate end? If you continually progress upward where do you eventually finish? To that question I do not think anyone ever got the final satisfying answer. Even Buddha himself hedged on the matter, and side-stepped out of the direct answer when the question was posed to him, taking the line that the important business was to get on with what we did know—*i.e.* the certainty of a chain of earthly lives—and leave the problem of the final retention of our individuality or our disappearance into blissful nothingness to the womb of the far future.

I suppose if you, my reader, ever get as far as this page you will want to know why on earth I am padding out this book with discursions of this nature—a book which I had promised to fill with words more or less relevant to the pictures of Ladakh.

My reason is that one wants to know a little about

the people at whose pictures one is looking—what they eat, how they live, what they think. And of what they think perhaps the most interesting point is what they think about the future after death. And, since the Ladakhi Tibetan is nominally a Buddhist, one obviously ought to have some kind of idea what Buddhism means, and to understand that, one has to know what Buddha's predecessors thought.

I do not know how many books there are on Buddhism, I only know that I have read at least a couple of dozen, and then touched only the fringe of the subject, for it is a vast one, and people really take the trouble to go into it with fairly open minds, wherein it differs from other religions, concerning which books are either violently abusive or hopelessly partisan.

A complete book the size of this one would give only an outline of Buddhism; the few pages which is all I will inflict upon you can give only an outline of an outline.

Buddha, as everybody knows, was a reformer; he was also an historical personage, and of what in India is called a royal family—probably we should say, at most, nobility. But he was an earnest thinker, and his line of thought was to try to find out why man was unhappy and suffering, and how this misery could be allayed.

He sought first to solve it in the traditional Indian

way, by asceticism and renunciation; for India, for all that it is essentially a material country, much concerned with the many cares of daily life, in many ways far more than our own so-called "material West," has also been always ready to cut adrift from everything and adopt the starkest asceticism.

Buddha gave up the inhuman austerities beloved of the Indian, who pays much reverence to men who mutilate themselves, abstain from the little decencies of life, and recline gracefully upon beds of rusty iron spikes, holding aloft withered arms and self-scarred limbs attained in their search for sanctity. But he did cling to the idea of renunciation of all that was superfluous—and in particular of the flesh.

And he meditated, which is always India's sovereign recipe for attaining holiness and wisdom. The fruit of his meditation was that the unending chain of lives which Hindu thought showed as the fate of the whole sentient creation was due to ignorance and desire—to the lust of being.

Life was miserable, and therefore misery could cease only if one ceased to live—*i.e.* to be reborn after death, either in this sphere or in the other spheres, for there are said to be six of them, those of gods, demigods, men, animals, ghouls and hells.

Thereafter he formulated rules of life which should produce this desired end—the "eightfold noble path" and the "precious jewels"—the whole consisting in the principles of right thought, right speech, right action. And one line that he inculcated particularly was the vast merit to be attained by renunciation of normal human life—marriage, householding, and the other activities of man. To withdraw oneself from all these, and to retire into seclusion to meditate, this was the best of all the ways to escape in time from the curse of rebirth which was the inevitable consequence of action, since the account could never be square at death—always there must be something wanting, something to expiate, something to make up which would demand yet another life, and the actions of that life would inevitably demand still a further one, and thus the wheel of lives would swing through all eternity.

It was doubtless as much above the heads of the majority of his hearers of those days as it is above the heads of most people to-day, but it took tremendous hold, eventually sweeping over the whole of India and Ceylon, and much of the adjacent countries and China.

The reasons were probably twofold. The first most noticeable feature was that it was a merciful and unfanatical creed, at a time when religion was anything but merciful. Man has not yet emerged from the state when he is ready to rejoice in torturing and killing those who dare to hold religious views different from his own; and Buddha lived over two thousand years ago.

Buddhism has never persecuted, and its whole spirit is one of brotherhood—between man and man, between man and animal, down to the lowest form of life. And that is of its essence attractive to the mass of humanity in its more sober moments—when its more primitive feelings are not being worked upon by oligarchies such as the Soviet, and autocracies like Prussia, with ends of their own to foster.

And the second reason was that it did offer some definite kind of plan for man to go on. There were more or less definite rules of life—beacons in the prevailing chaos of darkness: there was the happy mean between insane asceticism and unbridled self-indulgence, and that again appeals to the ordinary man, something normal and average; and, lastly, it raised the status of woman very notably.

But its inherent weakness killed it in the end, at least so far as India was concerned. It was too attenuated a theory, too much in the clouds, for the average man really to grasp. The average man wants something concrete to worship, something he can see and understand, something not too unlike himself or what he thinks himself to be—an idol or a more or less understandable deity. Buddhism provided neither.

But it did even worse. It made out that there was no such thing as a priest, that man stood on his own feet, so to speak. And this in a country where the priestly caste is born, not made—twice born—utterly above the rest of humanity, so that to strike a Brahman was a greater crime than to kill your brother. Financial loss is an unpleasant thing to face, loss of prestige and place is to many men even worse. And the final success of Buddhism would have meant both to the highest caste in India.

Thus inevitably there was collision between Buddhism and Brahmanism, and, in the end, Brahmanism carried the day, and Buddhism, for all practical purposes, vanished from India.

But before that happened there was a certain merging of the two, as one after another Buddhism adopted the practices of the older religion, so that the gods and the demigods filled the temples, and the rites and practices of Hinduism came back into their own.

It was this form of Buddhism that was introduced among the Tibetans and took root. It is not fair therefore to complain that the Buddhism of Tibet is not what Buddha taught, as though the Tibetan was responsible for the fact. It certainly is not—in fact it is rather hard to find Buddhism as one imagines it ought to be, or to find even the traces of it in the very monasteries, save only for the images and paintings of Buddhas and bodhisats sprinkled among those of the gods and demons.

Originally, I believe, untold centuries ago, the primal

religion of the Aryan race, who form now what we call the Indians, was monotheistic. But man, especially primitive man, wants tangible realities. Abstract conceptions of an Infinite Being who possesses all the attributes make no real appeal. And so one can imagine the rise of the three million deities who make up the Hindu Pantheon as conception after conception crystallized into stone and wood, and the Supreme Being's attributes of Protection and Mercy became the separate deity Vishnu, and his power of destruction was symbolized as the god Shiva—and so on.

Moreover, primitive man said that God or the gods were fertile; they produced things, and therefore they must obviously have female counterparts, since to primitive man the only agent for producing things, whether the reproduction of himself in the child or the production of his lambs and calves—even the crops of his fields—was differentiation of sex.

And so we find the appearance of the female deities—counterparts of the already crystallized male ones, their consorts—something again that man could understand.

Further, since life itself, its unceasing reproduction, was a mystery of all-absorbing interest to man, that also came in, and the worship of sex as sex—the worship of the reproductive powers of man and woman symbolized by the physical members—assumed a large share

—indeed sometimes absorbed the whole—of the religious stage, as in many places in India it does to this day.

Therefore Buddhism as it entered Tibet was but little removed from Tantric Hinduism, save that, in addition to the Hindu Pantheon—still further recruited by absorbing the minor clan and tribal deities of the various earlier peoples overcome by the Aryans as they slowly conquered India—there entered also half-forgotten, one-tenth-understood memories of Buddha's teaching, and the images and relics of Gautama, as Buddha was called in this world.

The main cause of Buddhism entering Tibet—which in those days, a few centuries after Christ, also included Ladakh—was two women, the joint wives of the King of Tibet. One was Chinese—for the connexion with China and Tibet has been close all through history—and the other was a Nepalese princess: the White and Green Taras as they are called to-day. Whether or not they quarrelled one does not know, but they had this much in common, that they were both anxious to see their mutual religion introduced into their new country. So at their request the king sent for Buddhist missionaries from India, and he and his people adopted the Law which, in a somewhat obliterated and disguised style, they have maintained ever since.

This was not the first appearance of Buddhism in

Ladakh, for a purer form of it had been introduced at the dawn of the Christian era by missionaries from India—the Mons—probably people of Kashmir, and traces of their rock-carvings may still be seen. But it vanished more or less entirely, and the Buddhism of Ladakh as we know it is that which came there from India via Tibet, and most writers speak of it as Lamaism rather than as Buddhism.

Buddhism had laid down the path of renunciation of the world for men and women alike, and monks and nuns were one of its most salient features. In Tibet therefore we find the monks and nuns—the "lamas" and "chumos." But from being merely recluses absorbed in meditation, the lamas have become very much what the priesthood of India has always been, save only that birth does not come into the question since the path of Buddhist monkhood or nunhood is open to all. But in other respects they have developed into what Buddha never intended them to be—the intermediaries between man and the supernatural beings, or rather those beings who have attained a sphere of life outside this visible human or animal one.

The so-called Buddhist of Ladakh worries very little about Gautama or Gautama's teachings except in so far as they form part of Lamaism. To begin with he does not concern himself much about religion at all, for, as he tells you, that is the business of the lamas—which, if you think it out, is a logical division of labour. The lama lives largely upon the layman, or upon land and property that he has obtained from the layman, and he ought therefore most certainly to justify himself by doing some kind of expert work.

The Ladakhi never goes to church in the sense that the Mussulman goes to his mosque or the Hindu to his temple. That, again, is the business of the lama, who holds services and reads the Buddhist scriptures written in the classical Tibetan, which very often he does not understand.

But the Ladakhi's working philosophy of life is, in a way, occupied with religion, in that he believes in the transmigration of his and every other being's soul. And therefore, strictly according to Buddha's precept, he does refrain from taking life, save only for the slaying of such domesticated animals as are necessary to give him the meat without which man cannot live in cold and high altitudes.

In Tibet proper, the fact that the killing of animals is a sin is got over by the lama's holding a special service for the animal to ensure that it is reborn immediately in a higher sphere, and therefore its killing, far from being a sin, becomes actually an act of merit, in that the creature's soul is helped up the ladder towards the attainment of Nirvana, the desired stage, where rebirth, and so misery, shall cease. In Ladakh I have not heard of this being done, and the matter is more simply settled by the butcher being always a Mussulman, upon whose soul, presumably, either there is no sin or, if there is, it does not matter.

For the rest, the practice of religion disturbs not the Ladakhi at all: once or twice a year he goes to the big festivals at the monasteries, which sometimes are also associated with fairs, and he gets his blessing and makes his offering to the head lama or to the Skushok, and comes away with a piece of blessed cloth pinned on to his quaint cap or fastened to the bosom of the woman's gown.

But what he really is concerned with is devils, who are a very potent and unforgettable factor in his daily life.

To most of us, devils are merely subjects of academic discussions, or sometimes convenient methods of describing people we happen to dislike. To the Ladakhi, however, who rubs elbows with them day and night throughout the year, they are something which has to be tackled seriously, as London, for instance, hunts rats, or India has perforce to grapple with the anopheles mosquito or the rabid dog.

CHAPTER
FIVE

LADAKHI RELIGION

CHAPTER FIVE

Ladakhi Religion

YOU see, when Padma Sambhava—thanks to the influence of the Green and White Taras—came into Tibet from India, with his little party of Buddhist missionaries, his precious yak-loads of Buddhist manuscript, and, surely, a heart full of missionary zeal, he did not come into conflict with any particular kind of religion as we know religions nowadays.

What he found was a fairly savage people, whose religious advance was at the Animist state, with a leaning towards the worship—or I suppose one should say the placation—of malevolent spirits.

Man has an instinctive belief in supernatural beings, and, for primitive man anyway, such beings always fall into two classes, the benevolent and the evilly disposed. Obviously, therefore, he has two lines of action open to him—to worship the benevolent, in the hope that they will protect him; or to pay court to the malevolent, on the chance of their leaving him alone. To primitive man, again, benevolence is at its best a negative kind of virtue. Primitive man worships strength, force and action, and in his mind these three qualities, judging by human analogies, are more often than not directed to the suppression, with more or less cruelty, of the weaker folk.

Moreover, the benevolent being is not likely to hurt you in any case, whereas the malevolent one is of his nature practically certain to make you feel his power. And so, as a rule, he concentrates his energies on placating the unpleasant spirits and the kind ones get either the leavings or maybe nothing.

Tibet was more or less solid in the matter, and under the leadership of the Bon priests directed its attention to keeping on the best possible terms with the evil spirits who swarmed in the country.

Some people—probably their enemies—accused the Tibetans of cannibalism; everybody accused them of sorcery, in which the accusations were probably better founded, for the old religion of Tibet was mostly made up of sorcery and black magic generally. The black-hat Bon priest's chief business in life lay, in fact, with devils.

Padma Sambhava, exponent of a faith which, originally anyway, did not take much count of devils—for all its subsequent impregnations with Tantric ideas—set out to combat the demons, and found that they, or rather their representatives the priests, were too strong for him. But he possessed in full measure the inherent gift of Hinduism—which was, as we have seen, the parent stock of Buddhism—the gift of compromise.

Instead of merely telling the devils they did not exist, he took them into his fold, and the already countless beings who filled his so-called Buddhist Pantheon were further augmented by the admission of the original deities and devils of Tibet. Thereafter he installed Buddha's image in the middle of the monasteries he founded, converted the local priests into monks—lámas, as they are called in Tibet—and, lo and behold! Tibet becomes a Buddhist country.

Not unnaturally it worked well; because, when you have been the central feature of a country for centuries and centuries, it would be cruelly hard to be told that you were a myth and did not exist. Any self-respecting demon would have to protest. But to be given a high-sounding Sanskrit name in addition to your own, and to be offered a place of honour in the temple, is quite another matter. In fact, had Padma Sambhava lived to-day he would most certainly have been one of the original founders of the League of Nations.

Two things, however, he did succeed in doing. First, he stopped human sacrifices, in which, in common with all other primitive races, the Tibetan indulged; and, second, he induced the people at large to adhere to Buddha's precept anent not taking animal life.

We see again thereafter the same line of thought being followed as had proceeded before. Buddha, who by now had, quite in defiance of his own teachings, been

—for all practical purposes—deified, was obviously a benevolent person, and therefore need not be thought about overmuch. The local devils, on the other hand, had, if anything, increased a little in importance.

Man as a whole is more afraid of what he cannot see than of what is visible. If the demons came out into the open you would probably be able to see their weak points, and be able to ridicule them, and, as everybody knows, ridicule is a most potent antidote to fear.

But when you can see only the places they live in, and merely hear the noise of their activities, they assume all sorts of qualities to which probably they have no right—much as in war a hillside on which you can see no sign of the enemy, only guessing his presence from the nasty "zip zip !" of bullets about your ears, is a far more terrifying thing to face than is the sight of a large mass of Huns drawn up in the open, who at least appear to be susceptible to bayonets and suchlike comforting tools. If you happen to catch the said Hun out in the open early in the morning cleaning his teeth, and if particularly he happens to be fat, with a hat three sizes too small, all sense of fear departs for ever. The devils know this and so keep under cover and use the lamas as their agents.

The Tibetan has thus a thorough fear of the demons, and does his continual best to keep in their good books by being obsequiously nice to their priests.

So as you ride on into Ladakh from Moulbekh, where we stopped, you will see anti-demon devices on all sides. You must remember the creatures swarm all over the place—that valley running up to your left is filled with them; the avalanches that come down from the snow above are their handiwork; the stone shoots that ignorant people like you and me put down to the action of rain and frost are, as the Tibetan knows, merely the demons throwing down rocks on somebody who has been incautious enough to emerge from his village on the wrong side of a *mane* wall.

The nasty cutting winds on the passes, which in conjunction with a blizzard may mean death to the traveller, are not, as one would think, the result of atmospheric depressions—or whatever the meteorologists call the phenomena governing winds—they are devils in actual form. And therefore along the hills on either side of a col the Tibetans put up little stone cairns, which at a distance look like men and frighten the devils away, more particularly if the cairns are adorned with a few strips of cloth and a twig or two of the holy *shukpa* tree.

Red paint is effectual too, if you plaster it heavily upon goats' horns and yaks' horns and display them conspicuously on your house or along the road.

The sudden violent spates which sweep down from these Ladakhi hills, where there is no vegetation to retard their pace, are most destructive. The gaunt hillsides are literally seamed with what appear to be trenches dug by the hand of man, but which are really cuts made by sudden spates. And these spates are not duc, as we might imagine, to the sudden release of hitherto dammed-up water from the melting snows—they are poured down by demons to destroy the fields, cattle and houses of those who have been incautious enough not to put up their prayer banners, and have left their praying wheels at home. Therefore you must defeat the devils if you would avoid the spates.

Padma Sambhava's great contribution to Tibet seems thus to have been the mystic verse, "*Om mane padme hum*," which has all the virtues. American patent medicines are not in it with this recipe. You inscribe it on stones, and pile up *mane* walls of them, and the devils flee. You carve he words on skulls of yaks in the nomad districts, pile up the skulls, and the devils of the high plateaux have to go miles round before they can get at you again.

You get the lamas to print them for you on little bits of rag and fly these on sticks over your house, and every time the wind flaps them the devils shudder and bolt.

You build little *chortens* at the entrance to the gorges, paint them red and fly a prayer flag or two, and the water-spate devils are held in leash. You get the lama to print with wood blocks a few hundred thousand repetitions of the verse on a roll of paper and put it into a brass roller, which you spin upon a stick as you walk, and again the demons are discomfited and leave you alone.

Lastly, while you sleep, if the wind is not flapping your prayer flags, you hope that the water of the little irrigation channel is steadily turning the water-wheel which contains a million or so "*Om manes*," and the demons are therefore harmless.

Moreover, you are actually gaining spiritual merit as well, and hoping for a higher rebirth after death. Only remember, the lama has to arrange it all for you, and if you cannot scare off the devils with all these means you must get the lama in person to read from the sacred books in your house.

For that is in actual practice the lama's chief business in Ladakh—the driving off of evil spirits. He is supposed, of course, also to be gaining merit for himself, and the world at large, by meditating in his monastery, but I think that is the lesser part of his work. You see, most of them, the red lamas, are the lineal descendants of the old black-hat priests of the Bon religion, which existed before the present Lamaism — or so-called Buddhism. And the black hat, whom you may still see at the great mystery plays, was primarily a sorcerer.

After death you are faced with the devil business

even more seriously, because unless you have climbed to the top of the ladder, and have already attained Buddhahood, with its consequent exemption from re-birth, your business is to get born again as quickly as possible, in some surroundings better than the ones you have left. The now disembodied spirit wanders round between the worlds seeking to be reborn—waiting for the psychological moment when it may enter the new body just beginning.

But always the demons are on the look-out trying to mislead it, to frighten it away from the proper path, so that it is left in the cold and darkness, wailing with fear and unable to find shelter. And the spirit that has neglected the lamas in its last life is in for a bad time, and will in the end find itself as the moving force of an about-to-be-born snake, or a beetle, or a lizard—or in one of the hells. There it will be put through an unceasing process of actual tortures—frozen and boiled alternately, cut to pieces with rusty saws and immediately repaired for the process to begin anew—or it may find itself reborn as a ghoul, to lead a Tantalus kind of existence, where it will have an enormous stomach, and suffer acutely from hunger and thirst, but with a throat so small that it can eat or drink nothing.

But if it is lucky it may find its way into the unborn body of the child of a Royal House—or even into the spheres of the gods or of the demigods, all of whom

"TAKE ME HOME, MUMMIE."
A scene at a Monastery Fair

lead a really happy existence over great intervals of time, until the swing of the wheel of life shall bring them to other fates, either to escape once for all from rebirths or, perhaps, if they have not conducted themselves as they should have, to be reborn as men, as animals, or in the hells.

And the real determining factor for man here again is merit, not that which he himself has accumulated, but that which he has allowed the lamas to accumulate for him. So far has Tibetan Lamaism departed from Gautama's teachings—Gautama, who taught that man was dependent upon himself alone, that man's own actions were the sole factors upon which depended his future.

The demons are invisible and therefore the more terrifying, but man does want something concrete to worship, and therefore the monastery chapels are filled with images of the gods—some of terrifying aspect, dog-toothed and stag-horned, myriad-armed and centipede-legged, red and blue and green and yellow —the gods and goddesses, mostly, of the Hindu Pantheon, with Tibetan names.

Religion therefore, as you can see, enters in some ways but little into the Ladakhi's daily life—but the lama enters it continually, at every turn.

As a result, however, the Ladakhi is a most unfanatical person, knowing nothing about his own religion and therefore caring little about that of others. He is, however, selfish, because what he knows as religion teaches him that his chief concern is with the accumulation of merit for himself. This trait of selfishness is strongly marked, and is perhaps the most unpleasing feature of the Ladakhi character. With us, "merit" is largely based on what we do for our neighbour—whatever the English world may have forgotten of the teachings of Christianity, the one lesson that is almost inborn is that of the Good Samaritan, and we do instinctively endeavour to adhere to the "second" commandment even if we do not consciously think much about the first.

I have said that the Ladakhi does not go to church in the sense that people of other religions do. But every house has its own little chapel, for all that the chapel may be only a wee niche in the big smoke-blackened room that serves as kitchen and living-room. There is enshrined the "*Lha*," the house-god, to whom offerings are made daily—little bowls of food and water, gifts of flowers—and his quarters are changed from time to time during the year according to the seasons.

Like most Ladakhi possessions he is essentially a traveller, living in a little shrine that can be carried on a man's back, or even hung at a man's belt—a little painted and gilded metal figure of one of the many deities—Avalokita, God of Mercy; Dukar, Goddess of Plenty; or any other of the three million or so inhabitants of the uppermost segment of the wheel of life.

Such, very very briefly, is the religion of Ladakh as it is to-day. Of lamas I will try to show you something in the next chapter—of their way of life, and of their dealings with the laity, on whom they really live.

Islam — the religion of Mohammed — has a certain hold in the country, more particularly in Leh itself and in the Shushot villages in the Indus Valley, and it is slowly extending, producing a strange effect, in that, the two extremes of polygamy and polyandry meeting, the resultant product seems to be monogamy. This is due probably to a mutual unconscious compromise in the many mixed marriages that take place, since the Mussulman husband refuses to share his wife with other men, and the Ladakhi woman objects to sharing her position with any others of her sex.

In some of the Dard villages of the Indus Valley we find a curious state of affairs, in that the religion changes at each generation, the children of Buddhists becoming Mohammedan and those of Moslems becoming Buddhists. I fancy that neither religion is taken very seriously at all by the Dards of these parts.

Leh has always been a Christian missionary centre ever since European influence has been established there. There have been both Catholic and Moravian missionaries, but only the latter now remain, and they probably owe their position to the most excellent medical work they have done. One of the main reasons perhaps for its popularity as a mission centre is that it seemed to offer a starting-point for mission work in the long-closed land of Tibet. Similarity of race, of speech and of religion would seem to point to it as an ideal training-ground for missionaries who hoped to go farther afield into Tibet proper.

But the number of Christians is small, and not on the increase in any notable quantity. I think that the most useful kind of mission would be a medical one, which, while doing untold good among the Ladakhis, whose knowledge of medicine may be described as *nil*, would at the same time set an example of what Christianity really stands for. Such an influence in this corner of the Empire, bordering on both Tibet and Chinese Turkestan, would to my mind be invaluable. But essentially such missions must be English, and of the best type—men such as we have seen in Kashmir.

It is possible after reading what I have written that one may be inclined rather to laugh at the Tibetan and his religious ideas. But that, I think, is never fair, unless the laughter be sympathetic and good-humoured. The Ladakhi really does believe in his gods and his demons, and more especially in the latter. And it always seems to me that in the first instance it is the matter of believing something which is of prime importance, rather than in what you believe. There are many people I have met who believe in nothing at all, except themselves, and I very much prefer the Ladakhi.

He is nominally a Buddhist—actually a Lamaist—and he understands next to nothing about either faith. But he is here in excellent company, for after reading many books by people who are really very learned, and are considered to be experts on the matter, from the amount they differed I came to the conclusion that neither they nor anyone else could really understand either system—not surprising, because, from what one can gather, even the earliest of Buddha's followers could not explain what Gautama did actually teach.

The Ladakhi is certainly ignorant, but then so are lots of other people in the world—people with very much less excuse for being so. He is superstitious, and when superstition and prejudice have vanished from Europe then, I imagine, we may be justified in thinking about plucking the motes from the Ladakhi's eyes.

On the other hand, he is a peacefully inclined person, and Peace—with a capital P—seems to be the one thing that everybody talks and writes about nowadays. I do not know if they have yet started broadcasting it.

But two notable things about his religious beliefs—his ignorance and his superstition—are that they do not render him cruel and they keep him extremely cheerful, and these two qualities seem to my possibly primitive mind worth a great deal more than much learning.

I have wandered into nearly every monastery I ever passed at one time or another. I have been courteously received. I have been shown round by lamas, who were anxious to explain all they could to the best of their ability, which unfortunately is not great as a rule. I have even had a religious service put on at a special hour so that I might take photographs of it. I do not know of any other form of religion that would do so much for a perfect stranger. And in nearly every case I have been offered tea and the usual apricots or walnuts of ceremony, while my following were regaled with a still larger meal.

So I must confess to a very great sympathy with the Ladakhi, even though I cannot believe in his much-feared demons, in whom I suspect, however, that he takes a certain amount of pride. It must be a great thing to have a bigger and more ferocious demon than the people in the next valley.

Lamaism may be a dreadfully degrading belief, but at least it does not produce the horrible cruelties and hatreds that less "degraded" thought seems to engender, and if one believes, as I do, in what I consider the essentially Christian theory of "Live and let live" —of tolerance, in other words—then there is still quite a lot to be said in favour of the Ladakhi and his quaint godlets, his myriad demons, and his red-clothed lamas.

CHAPTER
SIX

THE LAMAS

CHAPTER SIX

The Lamas

ALL along the road among the passers-by, and in every village in Ladakh, you will notice a number of men, in red, or once red, gowns, wearing either red or yellow caps, somewhat after the style of the ordinary Ladakhi headgear save that the yellow caps are high-pointed. You will, moreover, be struck by the respect with which your ponymen, and the inhabitants generally, treat these men, and remark that the ordinary Ladakhi salutation of "Julé," which is the equivalent of "Salaam" or "Good-day," is now prefixed with the word "Méme," which is translated to you as "Grandfather."

The red-gowned men do not look so very different from the ordinary folk; they are as unwashed, their clothes are generally just as poor and ragged; one thing only may you notice, if you be observant, and that is their foot-gear, which is high-toed boots with continuations of red cloth up to the knees, much like the boots of Greater Tibet but that the toe is blocked straight up for about an inch—a magnified edition of the American man's fashionable foot-wear.

They are lamas, and hence the respect with which

they are treated by the ordinary lay folk—monks of Lamaism, combining the functions of both priest and monk—theoretically recluses from the world and yet mingling with the laity, to whose spiritual needs they minister, after their fashion.

Buddhism, as we have seen, inculcated very strongly the teaching that the best spiritual path was that of renunciation of the world, of withdrawal into seclusion, there to pray and meditate, and so in time attain the desired goal of Nirvana—of freedom from rebirth.

After the fashion of the recluses of all time, the monks of Buddhism thought that the best localities to which to retire were the high and the waste places—the hills and the mountains. And therefore almost invariably you will find the monasteries built upon hills, upon hillsides in wild gorges or on isolated hillocks dominating the low river valleys. There is something fitting in this idea—something that appeals to man—this ascent into the high places in man's endeavour to draw nearer to his Creator, to detach himself from the myriad claims of normal human life. Just as man has always conceived of the mountains as the dwelling-places of the gods—so that Zeus was said to dwell upon Olympus, and Moses received the Commandments upon a mountain, and God Himself during His life on earth went up into a "high place alone" that He might be transfigured before His chosen disciples—so also has man felt that he who would seek God must retire into "a high place—alone."

The reason for the differentiation of the lamas' caps is that those wearing the red head-gear belong to the old unreformed sect of Ladakh, whereas those with the yellow caps are members of the new reformed church —the "Gelugpa," founded three centuries ago by Tsong Kapa in Greater Tibet.

The ideals of Buddhist monkhood were high—they embraced the ideals common to all monkhood: self-denial, abstinence from the world, celibacy and meditation. Inevitably these ideals deteriorated—inevitable when the religion which fostered them had, as we have seen, fallen so far from its first high promise as to become almost indistinguishable from the degraded Tantric Hinduism.

Tsong Kapa, filled with thoughts of the old faith as he conceived Buddha had intended it to be, looked round upon the monks and nuns, to find that there was very little left of the ideals, save only that they still shaved their heads, that as a rule they did not get married officially, and that they lived more or less in communities. They did, moreover, insistently adhere to Buddha's precept of living upon charity, though in a way utterly remote from Gautama's conception of the alms bowl of the religious, whose simple needs—handfuls of rice, a few little wheat-cakes—were to be given to him daily by the laity so that he might be absolved from the necessity of working with his hands, and thus have the more time to devote to religion. Tsong Kapa therefore set to work to reform the monks, and for a time he undoubtedly succeeded. Moreover, like all men who have any understanding of human nature, he set value upon symbols. It is left to the fanatics of a materialistic civilization to say that there is no value in symbolism of dress or indeed of any form. All will agree that a man may be intrinsically as saintly in a costume of jazz silk as in the rough black or brown of a Benedictine or a Franciscan, just as a soldier *may* be an excellent soldier despite a rat-catcher get-up. Nevertheless, taking men in the mass, the outward wearing of a garment which really symbolizes something will produce a vast amount of inward grace that would not otherwise be there.

Saffron is the colour immemorially associated in India with the idea of renunciation of the world, and Buddha bade his followers clothe themselves in saffron as a sign that they had renounced the world. Tsong Kapa, seeking regeneration at the fountain-head, told his reformed monks to follow the old custom, and to change their robes of gaudy red for yellow.

Here again, however, tradition had its way—the people at large associated lamas with red gowns, in the same way as Jones, Smith, and Robinson, and their wives, connect black and a clerical collar with the minister of religion, so that the most that Tsong Kapa could achieve for the rank-and-file of his monks was that their caps should be yellow, and of shape somewhat different from the old red ones.

For the hierarchy he contrived more yellow, and a Gelugpa "gelong"—who is what we might call a canon, or a prior, with a touch of doctor of divinity about him, since he has to pass examinations to get the degree—wears a gold-and-yellow undergarment below his red robe, while sometimes a Skushok of the Gelugpa will wear yellow from head to foot. One small community of lamas in Zanskar wears all-yellow garments, but for the rest, apart from the caps, the red and yellow sects are clothed alike in red.

But Tsong Kapa did instil a great many of his ideas, and the yellow lamas are notable for leading lives somewhat nearer to the original models of Buddha's time, cleaner, less worldly, more erudite, on the whole, than their red brethren.

They are, moreover, in closer touch with Lhassa, which is to Lamaism what Rome is to Catholicism, and the Dalai Lama, who is to Buddhism what the Pope is to the Roman Church, and who is invariably of the yellow sect.

A lama is made, not born. Anyone may become a lama, even in late life—though more usually he enters monkhood as a child, even as a baby, and to have a child become a lama is probably as much to the Ladakhi family as to the Southern Irish family would be the entry of a son into the priesthood.

You meet the novices in all the monasteries, and their early education is severe, for Lamaism believes very firmly in the use of the rod to prevent the spoiling of the children. From this one can see how prehistoric and akin to the English public school, in some ways, is this faith of a forgotten land.

But, apart from this excellent recipe, viewed from our standards the rest of the lama's education is poor. He learns to read and to write, but not, save in rare cases, to understand what he reads or writes—the majority of his instructors themselves could not teach him that. He learns to patter charms and to intone the Buddhist scriptures—the Tengyur and the Kangyur—one of one hundred and eight large volumes, the other of, so far as I remember, sixty-three tomes.

He learns the ritual of the services, but is generally ignorant of the identity of the myriad gods and bodhisats whose images and paintings fill his monastery. He learns also to play the religious instruments—the big warming-pan-shaped drums, the little clarinets, the great telescopic brass and copper trumpets, six or seven or eight feet long. He learns also to spin the "*dorjés*," the thunderbolt symbols of Lamaism—which are the main mark of the lama; learns also to play the little double-sided drums, which are turned in the hand and so beaten by a small weight on a string as they twist backwards and forwards—little double drums, of which the best are made from the brainpans of two human skulls, and like the *dorjés* are mighty weapons against demons.

He is taught also how to make the ceremonial offerings of *chang* and barley, to build the pyramids of butter and parched grain which are piled up on festival days; learns too the charms against evil spirits which will form so much of his work later on when he goes out among the laity.

And you meet him sometimes in company with an old lama—going out to celebrate a marriage or a funeral—bearing the little brass shrined images or the tomes of the scriptures, acting in fact as acolyte, and so learning the practical side of the business.

Then for such as show aptitude there are the arts and crafts to be learned—the printing of the scriptures by use of wooden and metal blocks, the fashioning of images in metal or wood or plaster, the painting of the wall frescoes, without which no monastery would be complete.

Again, there are horoscopes to be learned, the manner of selecting auspicious days for weddings, the selection of names for children, the choice of methods of disposing of the dead—an important business this, upon which may depend the hereafter of the departed spirit.

And in time the keen-eyed little boy—none save the physically perfect is accepted as a lama, a fact which may account for a certain amount of racial degeneration, since a lama is or should be celibate—may rise to being a gelong, may come to be head of a sub-monastery—but never can he become a "Skushok," who is, in a way, what we should call an abbot, but very much more so.

A "Skushok" is born, not made. There is no restriction as to his family, no sign of the Hindu theory of caste—it is a matter of the spirit. A Skushok—which I believe is a term peculiar to Ladakh, meaning as it does merely a noble—is in greater Tibet termed a "Living Buddha," and the Dalai Lama is the greatest example of what in Ladakh is called a Skushok.

A Skushok after death can be reborn only as a Skushok—he is free of the chain of life; reborn only to serve the world, not for his own regeneration, for he has already attained perfection.

His spirit is that of Buddha, of a personified attribute of Buddha, or of some famous bodhisat.

When, therefore, a Skushok dies those about him listen earnestly in the hope that he may give them some clue as to where his spirit will reincarnate, which he may or may not do.

SPITOK GOMPA.

This Monastery is typical of the way in which most of these buildings in Ladakh are perched on a hill.

Thereafter they wait for a time, which must not be less than a matter of ten months but which may be considerably longer—may run to several years—and then they set out to seek for the babe or child whose human form conceals the immortal spirit of the living Buddha. They may have some clue to guide them as to the locality, some clue caught from the dying words in his last incarnation—or they may be dependent solely upon the auguries of their sacred books.

Eventually they will gather together several children whose birth has occurred later than the minimum period necessary since the Skushok last changed his body—interesting, this, since it implies a belief that the soul enters the embryo body from the moment of conception. All these children are possible inheritors of the Skushok soul, since they have been gathered together as fulfilling the necessary qualifications with regard to time and place of birth, physical indications peculiar to the particular living Buddha whom they seek—for instance in the case of the Dalai Lama they look for, among other signs, slight excrescences on the shoulders representing the extra arms of Amithaba, the Buddha of Boundless Light, and miraculous portents at time of birth as expected from the readings of the sacred books considered apposite to the case in hand.

The children are then shown possessions of the late Skushok—his robes, his insignia, his *dorjé* and drums, and so on—and when one or other of the children evinces recognition of some or all of these, possibility is converted into certainty.

The mother retains the child for such time as may be necessary for its upbringing, after which—perhaps at the age of four or five or six—the little Skushok is taken to his monastery and placed in the care of a selected tutor, whose work is to instruct him in such business of life as he has forgotten—to read and write—to learn again his duties in the charge which he has held for so many centuries.

I had the fortune to meet a child Skushok, him of Spitok, near Leh—to my mind one of the most pleasing and the most monastic monasteries in Ladakh. He was a delightful and good-looking little boy of about eight, with charming manners and very human. In his last incarnation he was very keen on photographs—a fact of which I reminded him when I was taking his photograph and that of others in the monastery. But quite apart from this he was boyishly interested in my cameras and boyishly enthusiastic when I let him make a couple of exposures with my small film camera—they were of his tutor, for whom he seemed to entertain a very genuine regard. By now, I expect, the resultant prints are framed in his room along with the many photographs and pictures he had gathered in his previous incarnation, when he travelled far afield in India and rode upon an elephant at Delhi, and was, I think, present at Lord Curzon's durbar.

One thing I have never been able to fathom, and that is what happens to the bad Skushok, of whom Ladakh has possessed its examples and of whom it has one at present. The fate of the bad man or woman is rebirth in the hells or in some much lower stratum, such as that of the animals. But a Skushok can never be born as aught but a Skushok, and the poor monks of Triksé monastery, who have a Skushok whom they call very bad, have an awkward future before them, since for all eternity he will be abbot of Triksé.

In this life he is an exile in some corner of Tibet, out of favour with everybody for his misconduct. It must be said in his defence that they did not run him to earth until, with no desire whatever to enter the monastic life, he was eighteen or twenty, and in the end they were unable to keep him in the monastery at all. But they are faced with the dilemma either of admitting that their recognition of him was wrong—rather an impossible precedent to create—or of putting up with him in this life and in all his future earthly lives.

The lamas do not by any means all live in monasteries. Large numbers of them live out in the villages and partake of the ordinary activities of the laity, sometimes even, in lax communities, to the extent of getting married. They also work with their hands in matters connected with the monastery, such as tilling the fields and trading; and I have met parties of monks bringing back loads of wool from the flocks in the Chang Tang to Santanling monastery, far away in the Nubra—brawny, yellow-capped, smiling folk, with whom I have hob-nobbed under the passes, shoeing their ponies by the wayside, with their little brass shrines propped up on a boulder near by.

I mentioned as one of the important businesses of the lama the question of deciding as to the disposal of the bodies of the dead—whether burial shall be by burning, by exposing to wild birds and beasts, or by throwing into the river. That of exposure, which is much practised in Greater Tibet, is said to be an act of merit for the deceased, and is based upon the story of one of Buddha's earlier lives, who, meeting a tigress which for lack of food was unable to give milk to her cubs, offered himself as food and was duly killed and eaten. There is supposed to be great virtue attached to such a funeral, but it is rarely if ever practised in Central Ladakh, where burning is the more usual rule. In the higher plateaux, such as the Chang Tang, where there is no wood, exposure to animals is said to be much used.

Sometimes, however, the body, which is always bent double, made into a bundle, and retained thus in the house for some days, is thrown into the river, and this—if decided upon by the lama—is always looked upon as a very untimely fate, with the most evil probabilities for the future. There is probably a connexion between it and the old Ladakhi method of execution, which consisted in binding a stone about the criminal's neck and casting him into one of the many torrents—a method doubtless evolved in order to keep within the Buddhist tenet prohibiting the shedding of blood.

Once the body has been burnt, the ashes and bones are pounded into little shapes and, after being kept one year in the house, placed in one of the many *chortens* which fringe the Ladakh villages—owned generally in common by groups of families, or by monasteries for their monks. The lamas hold services for the deceased on certain days after death. The number of such services, and the number of lamas who perform at them, is naturally proportioned to the rank and wealth of the deceased and the amount which the relatives are prepared to pay.

The lama also acts to a great extent as the doctor, since illness is primarily attributable to the action of evil spirits, and these are the province of the lama. Spells, incantations, and suchlike are therefore the proper method of curing disease, but the modern Ladakhi is inclined to prefer a Western doctor if he can get one, and the European traveller is nearly always besieged by people seeking medicine or dressing for wounds.

Speaking from personal experience I have found the

lamas of Ladakh extraordinarily ignorant of their own religion. Some people have told me that this is due to a desire not to explain matters to Europeans, but I do not believe this for one moment. I think it is simply that they themselves do not know. I have found them always most easy to get on with, childishly interested in modern scientific instruments—cameras and the like—and only too ready to show one everything there is to see. They would not be likely, therefore, to protest ignorance as to the names and attributes of images, and I have actually had two or more lamas arguing before me as to the name of this or that image or painting.

That the lama system on the whole holds back the country, I think there can be no doubt. To condemn the pick of your male population to celibacy must have a retrograde influence; there did not seem to be such importance attached to the physical perfection of such nuns as I saw, but the men were always good specimens. Moreover, to have a large proportion of the race in what is undoubtedly a parasitic existence is again bad for progress.

On the other hand, it does undoubtedly help to keep down the population within the limits of what the country can support, for emigration is useless to the Ladakhi, who does not thrive at low altitudes. The Balti, his Mussulman neighbour of the West, does emigrate, even if only temporarily, to India, where he is to be found working in large numbers on the hill roads. But he lives at an altitude which is, on the average, considerably lower than that of Ladakh, and he is, moreover, a Mussulman, and as such more adaptable to life in India.

If, however, the lama is at all responsible for the generally pleasing character of the Ladakhi, then I suppose there is something to be said for him, but I think that this is unlikely; it is the character of a people that is usually reflected in its priesthood rather than that of the priest in the people.

But that the lama and his institutions are picturesque no one who visits Ladakh can deny, and I think picturesqueness is an asset which it is becoming more increasingly the fashion to overlook, so insistent are we nowadays on the question of a materialistic "efficiency."

CHAPTER
SEVEN

THE MONASTERIES

CHAPTER SEVEN

The Monasteries

THE Ladakhi word for a monastery is "Gompa," the reason for the term being that, according to Gautama's precepts, monasteries are, or should be, built in solitary places, apart from the rest of the world. As I have already mentioned, they are in general built upon isolated hills in side valleys, or if in the vicinity of a village then upon the highest point it is possible to find.

You can generally tell a monastery from far off because, firstly, it is almost always the biggest and best-constructed building in the locality, and secondly, it is invariably known by poles upon the roof, from which droop streamers of yaks' tails—these last being considered very potent against demons. More often than not there are several extra large and imposing *chortens* in the vicinity.

Convents, in our sense of the term, are not to be found in Ladakh; the nuns, when there are any, live in separate buildings attached to the monasteries. The life of a nun is in many ways comparable to that of the religious we call "lay sisters" in Europe. She takes a very minor part in any religious services—about equivalent to that of the congregation in Europe—and she is chiefly engaged in much more menial tasks—cooking, sewing, etc.—as may be necessary for the monastery.

Each monk should live in his own cell, and in some monasteries this is properly adhered to, so that he has his own little set of rooms, approached by a separate stair or ladder.

In the interior of the monastery are always to be found at least two large rooms—the first, which if there are two storeys is more usually on the lower, forming the monastery library, where in rows of pigeonholes repose the sacred books. They are not books in our sense of the term, but rather the *pothis* of India—bundles of printed or written sheets bound up between two wooden boards, probably carved and perhaps lacquered, so that when the binding string is undone any sheet may be withdrawn. The whole is then generally wrapped in a covering of silk.

On the walls of this apartment are mu al paintings, and for the most part these will depict Buddha and his disciples, saintly lamas of the order; more rarely there may be one or two pictures of the gods.

In the second room, the "Lha Kang" or gods' house, will be the various images of those deities specially worshipped in the monastery. And here one gets a true bird's-eye view of Lamaism, and realizes the intricate structure that has risen on the simple base of Buddhism.

As you enter, on the wall containing the entrance and facing the altar will be, as a rule, the paintings of the hells surmounted by the gods of the lower regions, easily distinguished by their blue tint and the rather beastlike heads, heavy jaws furnished with the teeth of wild animals and blazing round eyes—many-armed beings, with each hand grasping a weapon or an instrument of torture.

The chief figure in the centre of the row, which usually consists of six, is, I believe, the Tantric representation of Ishwar, called Vargchuk. In common with many of the deities he is represented as three-eyed, the third eye being in the centre of the forehead—again a borrowing from Hinduism—and is usually blue, though I have seen him depicted also in red.

Often he is clothed in a leopard-skin and with a snake girt about him, while his four arms brandish insignia of divinity—the sword, the conch, the chakra, the *dorjé*. His wife, more often represented as green in colour, with similar doglike human features, is embracing him, and sometimes also proffering him a bowl which may or may not be shown as containing blood. Both figures are heavily adorned with jewellery, and with necklaces of skulls and heads.

Beneath their feet and beneath the feet of the other deities writhe pygmy figures of men, and also of animals. The men and women are generally in process of being tortured, and I must say appear to support their sorrows with an expression of comparative content, even with smiles, which is surprising since they are being roasted and frozen, slain and dismembered, while their " innards " are generally displayed in festoons to form a background to the fresco, or are twisted as garlands round the necks of the minor deities.

The blue gods are ferocious-looking beings, more particularly the centre one, while the female deities are more like our conception of the Greek harpies than of anything else. But a yellow-cap gelong with whom I once made friends, and who was at great pains to show us over his little monastery, and with whom I was able to talk for a long time, was insistent on the fact that this dog-faced, blue-headed gentleman was the kindest and nicest of all the hierarchy, and positively loved the little writhing human figures whom he was torturing only for their own ultimate good. In fact I came away with the idea—possibly right, possibly wrong—that he was intended to represent the supreme and complete happiness to which all would in time attain, when, in lieu of being only a magpa or else possessing merely a third share (approximately) of a wife, each man would be as the gods, having a complete and obviously loving wife of his own.

On the walls to right and left are more frescoes ; there is no inch of wall which is not covered with colour, and on either side one passes up from pictures of the hells and of the demons till one comes by transition to quiet-faced bodhisats and lamas in attitudes of meditation, each picture generally with some little story, which the lama in charge may or may not know. These paintings get very conventional and show the type of seated shaven figure which we associate with Buddhism all the world over.

And so we reach the altar at the farther end, fronted by tables bearing myriad little brass lamps burning melted butter through their smoky little wicks and brass bowls containing offerings of holy water, handfuls of grains, pyramids of coloured butter and flowers, while the air is heavy with the scent of burning joss-sticks brought from China via Lhassa.

The central figure above the altar may or may not be Buddha, but invariably there will be a big attendance of the more popular deities, some of whose pictures we have already seen and some of which are veiled for the greater part of the year—exposed to view only for one or two great festivals. People who are sensitively prudish probably feel glad that they are veiled, for statues are more striking to the eye than are wall-paintings done in the Lamaist style, where the wealth of ornamentation and detail is so great that one has to study them for a long time before one can even make out the separate figures of men or animals which make up the whole.

If there be a Skushok in the monastery, then in the very centre before the altar will be his throne, carved and gilded—a throne closed in in front like a desk, and on the table part will be his insignia—his *dorjé*, his little skull drums, his holy water-pot with the high peacock feathers, and his cup for the ceremonial tea-drinkings which alternate with the services.

On either side are the low seats of the lamas, with a higher one at the altar end for the head lama—the prior—and facing him—the lamas sit sideways to the altar—that of the novice master.

The seats are low—only a few inches in height—for the lamas squat on them on rugs and cushions, and before each is his little low Chinese tea-table, on which he places his sacred books and his bowl for tea or *chang*.

Before some of the low tables will be standing the instruments which serve the choir and which are played by certain lamas during the services.

On the carved and lacquered pillars, which as a rule support the roof (the arch is unknown in Ladakh and I think also in Greater Tibet), hang the masks used in the mystery plays—those of the more important deities only if the monastery has many masks; in other cases the majority of those they possess, even down to the skull masks of the ghouls.

The lighting as a rule is poor, usually being derived

only from the single door and from skylights—though I know one or two *gompas* where there are also side windows in the main chapel.

Behind the altar there is always a way round, built sometimes as a separate passage in almost complete darkness, and here you will frequently find the older statues, less gaudy as a rule, and generally containing one or more representations of Buddha. The object of the passage is, I think, to enable people to circulate round the altar—the same as the "*pradakshina*" of Hindu temples. In Hinduism—for Tibetan Lamaism drew greatly from the parent source—there is much virtue attributed to walking round any sacred object, always provided you walk in the same way as the sun—right-handed. We ourselves have still the same idea, as seen in the custom ruling the direction in which wine is passed round a table.

From the beams of the flat ceiling depend painted banners of silk—the gift of various donors. These *tankas*, as they are called, are often very beautiful—miniature replicas of the various mural paintings one meets—and are frequently very old, for in this bone-dry atmosphere of Ladakh such things last almost for ever though they may be smoke-begrimed and greasy.

There is a distinct air of mystery about a *gompa* chapel, and personally I have found it a friendly air, despite the myriad demons upon the walls. I suppose places of congregation inevitably come in time to reflect something of the mental atmosphere of the people who gather there, and the mental atmosphere of the Ladakhi, be he layman or monk, is, as I have endeavoured to make clear, friendly to all—devoid of all fanaticism.

But the air of mystery is apparent, and strikes all who come, I think—save only those who can see nothing at all in any person, place, or thing unless these be swept and cleansed up to the standards of the Ideal Home. If you go in that frame of mind, then of course any *gompa* will disillusion you straight away, for, with rare exceptions, the *gompas* are as dirty as you would expect them to be from the appearance of their guardians.

It is generally easy to recognize at first sight whether a monastery belongs to the red or yellow sect, from the images and pictures around it. But I know one red *gompa* at Shushal in the Chang Tang country which it is impossible to class unless you discover its parent house. Even the solitary lama in charge of it gives you no clues, since he wears neither red nor yellow cap—only his own hair, uncut, matted, and further lengthened with long plaits of yak hair, coiled upon his head in the fashion of a Hindu Rishi of old.

Inside, flanking the altar at Shushal, stand images of red and yellow lamas, and Buddha's usually detached and placid statue, with the hands folded in meditation, has got mixed up with the more normal representation of the blue god of hell, although the conventional yellow tint of Gautama has been retained. They cover the central figures with a large veil, leaving only the Buddha's head and the green lady's face smiling at you over the top, and someone—I think at a later date—has embellished Buddha's hairless visage with a large moustache.

But such mixtures are rare, and that of Shushal may be due to the fact that the Chang Tang people are rather primitive—the Ladakhi of Central Ladakh looks down upon them as semi-savage, which in truth they are, for their life is hard and devoid of much that even the Ladakhi would call necessary comfort. The Chang Tang woman as a rule, for all that she lives in a climate far colder than that of the Indus Valley, wears only one gown instead of the over- and undergowns, and does not sport the tight-fitting trousers without which the lady of Ladakh would never be seen. Moreover, like that of the women of the Nubra, her loose gown fastens badly, or more often not at all, above the waist, and nobody thinks anything of it; so that the Ladakhi strictures about these people being somewhat uncivilized are perhaps not unfounded.

Should the monastery be the seat of a Skushok you will visit also his own special suite of rooms, generally very clean and well kept; and beside his private altar

—a miniature replica of the big one below, though with fewer images and paintings—you will see the various items which he has gathered during the course of many earthly lives—for Skushoks are, after all, men, and, like more mortal men, have also hobbies in their spare time.

The Skushok of Santanling in the Nubra, for example —a personage of note in Ladakh—is an artist in his off moments, an artist of the Chinese school, which he studied for many years in Lhassa. Not only does he paint little water-colours on rice-paper with Chinese brushes and paints—vivid little pictures embellished with a wealth of detail—but he also does wall-frescoes, and the whole of his room at Sumur is gay with a floral pattern from his own hand.

The Spitok Skushok concentrates on photographs and toys. He has endless photographs of the places visited in the last incarnation—after photography had come into vogue—photographs of Delhi and Kashmir, groups of notables in India, enlargements of himself, pictures of his lamas; and flanking these are clockwork animals and a delightful rubber pigeon of the kind that children love to play with in their baths. The pigeon has a special place of honour alongside the skull drums.

Here in the sunlit room—Skushoks seem to like the sunlight—he reads and meditates, and prays for the well-being of mankind and for the happiness of all the sentient creation. Here also he transacts the details of the worldly business which he has to shoulder along with his more important spiritual tasks; interviews the *gompa* stewards with their accounts of the monastery lands and money, and receives his visitors, of whom he has many, from mere globe-trotters like ourselves to people who seek his advice on matters of real weight.

Upon the topmost flat roof of the monastery will be a raised plinth which, by the addition of a few rugs and cushions and a lacquered tea-table or two, can be converted into a sitting-out place, where the Skushok can bask in the sunshine of the spring and autumn months, looking out from his eyrie over the broad lands which the monastery has accumulated from past kings and rulers.

Ladakh is dotted with monasteries, large and small. Hardly a village of any note but has its *gompa*. But the smaller ones are not parent houses; they are only offshoots of the larger ones and do not generally support more than one or two lamas. Nor is there any territorial connexion between them; far and wide you find the little monasteries that belong to larger ones, perhaps a hundred—perhaps more—miles away.

And sometimes a monk will be sent into a remote district to restore some half-forgotten, half-ruined little *gompa*, with often no village for miles. One such I knew in the Nubra district—the *gompa* of Ensa—cut off from the nearest village, for months at a time, by the vast torrent that pours down from the melting Siachen glacier in the summer months.

The lama lived there alone, a travelled man, who had been much to Lhassa, and had also visited India and seen Calcutta and journeyed, as he told me with gusto, in a "*terain!*" He had a thankless charge, for not only was his monastery very remote from human habitations, but, also, it had been founded upon a hill-terrace under which passed a spring, so that the wall-paintings were flaking off in a most un-Ladakhi way, owing to damp, and the pillars leant at uncomfortable angles.

He did not dwell in the monastery itself, in which he was wise, but in a neighbouring building, planted upon a firm rock outcrop. And there, scorching in summer and snowbound in winter, he lives, year in, year out, with little company; sleeping in a niche in the wall, by his little fire; with his few books; his table supporting his *dorjé*, his drums, and his most precious possessions—the ceremonial drinking-cups, fashioned from human brain-pans, and his trumpet, bound with silver, which he himself had made from a human thigh-bone, cut with his own hands, from a chance-found corpse.

Judging by what he told me, he was rather despondent at the task laid upon him; the monastery was built in an impossible place and, moreover, was too remote to hope for much financial help from the laity. But he was cheerful and hospitable, in the usual lama way, and he produced very dainty Chinese teacups for us. Buttered tea always offends my stomach, and I think that had it been served in the tops of human skulls—however much I might lean to the Buddhist theory that the body is nothing more than a suit of clothes, to be changed from time to time—I should have experienced worse pangs than ever. Which shows how potent an affair is the imagination, for the cups were very nice and clean, albeit the bone was stained with some red dye.

Dogs are generally a feature of the *gompas*, and if you do not know your monastery it is well to approach with a strong stick, grasped ready for action, since the Tibetan mastiff is a large beast, with a temper not at all uncertain. Quite the contrary, in fact, since he has been taught for generations to ask no question but go straight for anyone he does not know. The monastery dogs are generally bigger and better fed than those in the houses, and could be really quite dangerous. But they are never pets; they are mercenary soldiery, treated in the same way as the Roman rulers used, doubtless, to treat the Goths and Visigoths and barbarians generally.

Inside the monastery, however, you may often find a real pet, more particularly if there is a Skushok in residence. Every Skushok I have met always owns one or more Lhassa terriers, little curly-haired, somewhat puglike animals, with the round head and protruding eyes that captivated the heart of the Victorian lady.

They are generally very friendly little beasts, ready to play with anyone, and this trait of dog-loving appeals to me in the Skushoks. The artist one of Santanling has, moreover, a trick of inserting a little inset of a dog in most of his pictures, which gives them a very human appeal—the little Lhassa terrier pawing at the silk skirts of the lady who is drinking tea with what is, evidently, a representation of a Chinese "knut," which is a favourite subject of the Sras Skushok when he turns his hand to lighter work as a change from mural pictures in chapels and elsewhere.

I have tried to show you that Ladakh holds a vast amount of fascination—the charm of wild hills and of wide spaces, of snow-capped peaks and great rock gorges, of quaint people, quaint customs and unfamiliar animals. But to some of us not the least of its charm is the interior of the monasteries—the images, the paintings, the atmosphere of the dim-lit chapels, with the heavy scent of incense and the half-seen representations of the gods and demons in the shadows.

Whatsoever you may believe, unless you happen to be a genuine materialist, you also will, I think, find all this fascinating. For when you look at it, if you have in you some curiosity about your fellow-beings, you will ask yourself what it all means, and you will begin to think—which is always a fascinating process. You will try to understand, not so much the system of Lamaism, but the workings of the spirit of the men who conceived it in their endeavours to find out what lies behind this visible world—their seekings after the infinite. And whatsoever you may believe, provided always that you believe in something, you will find unfailing interest in trying to fathom it all, to get at the realities behind the myriad representations of inhuman, semi-human, and super-human beings whose pictures and images are to be found on all sides.

To me, for one, this attempt to understand men of other races, and of thoughts other than my own, is a pursuit that never palls and never fails to charm, however little success I may achieve in my endeavours.

CHAPTER EIGHT

VILLAGE LIFE

CHAPTER EIGHT

Village Life

THE Ladakh villages are another feature which lends a quaint charm to this altogether quaint country. One book which I read, an account of a trip to Leh, made much mention of elves and gnomes, and the comparison was a happy one. There is something gnomelike in these people: the funny, peaked caps, at a distance, give one an idea of the conventional pictures of the fabled inhabitants of forests and mountains.

The villages, too, give one the same impression; the more so, perhaps, after some long and rather tiring march through rock gorges and over waste spaces, clambering over the rocks of giant moraines, or swinging along just above the torrents of the rivers. Suddenly you round a corner, or emerge at the mouth of a defile, and, lo! before you, perhaps almost under your feet, perhaps planted high above you, you see a huddle of quaint buildings, clinging around a central hill, crowned with the whitewashed, red-barred edifice of a monastery, and approached by a long avenue of *chortens* and *mane* walls—for these are always the first signs of life as you near human habitations—welcome sights at the end of the day's march.

Little huts, low and flat-roofed, are built in tiers up the sides of a steep, cliff-like hill, dotted here and there with the white *chortens* and red spires that surmount the more superior ones—spires made up of a series of thirteen red-painted rings, to signify the thirteen ages of this present world. White prayer-banners fluttering in the breeze, and long cords knotted with strips of coloured cloth between the poles of the prayer-flags, press the wind into the service of men's souls.

Above these again there may be a ruined castle or two, remnants of the old fighting days that have now passed away; freebooters' holds and feudal castles, destroyed either in the long Balti wars or, later, by the conquering Dogras when Zorawar Singh first captured Ladakh for his master, the Raja of Jammu.

Mud-built houses on mud-faces of hills, ruined castles and cliff-hung dwellings, that seem almost to be caves; twisting water-channels hung on the scarps; high monastery, with its streamers of yaks' tails; and on the tortuous paths, that snake up and down the hills, slow-moving figures, in elf-like garments—your first impression is that of a picture from some fairy-book.

And yet, perhaps, lower down, especially if it be the late spring or summer, there will be a wealth of green to affect the prevailing red-brown and yellow tones of the houses above and the scarred cliff-sides; perhaps a long vista of little terraced fields, all stone-walled—for Ladakh is full of stones and the first step in making a field is to clear the ground of the bigger stones, which are then piled up into walls, either to demarcate the field or to terrace it up the slope.

From the hidden glaciers pour down the silver streams of water which convert the dull expanse of arable ground into a carpet of emerald; field after field of waving, bearded barley and, perhaps, in the lower reaches, clusters of fruit trees—mulberry and apricot, apple and walnut.

Moving about in the fields you see the figures of women in dull, ragged garments and gaudy *peraghs* of turquoise, with conical baskets upon their backs, laden with fruit, or maybe manure, or perhaps with that most treasured and somewhat rare possession, a Ladakhi baby.

The women do much of the field work in Ladakh, for, along the main routes anyway, the men are more often occupied in their immemorial trade of carrying. Ladakh lies athwart the Central Asian trade route, and its people have been carriers from the dawn of history. From April until late November you meet the men on the road with their little ponies, their dzos, and higher up with their yaks, laden with the bales of Central Asia, or the neat-packed cases of kerosene oil, the cotton goods of Bombay and Manchester, and the cheap hurricane lamps of Mr Hinks, of the U.S.A., or of his still cheaper imitators in the Fatherland.

So old and well established is the custom that it is officially recognized and organized to-day, in that each village or group of villages has to provide its quota of men and animals to convey merchants and travellers at fixed rates, from stage to stage. As a matter of fact, they do not always adhere to the rates or stages, preferring often to take up contracts to transport merchandise over a long journey, at a slightly lower average rate, rather than hold to their right of going not more than one day's march at a somewhat higher rate of pay.

I have met Dras men on the Saser Pass, two hundred and fifty miles from their homes; Shushot men on the way out to Yarkand, which is nearly four hundred miles beyond the Nubra; Purigpas from Kargil on the Khardong Pass, beyond Leh; Nubra men in the Chang Tang. But, normally speaking, the "*res*," as the organized transport is called, is forced to go only one stage from their homes. Economically, this is a good arrangement, for thus no grain or fodder has to be carried for the animals, since they are back next day at latest, perhaps even the same night, and so can carry their full load of two hundred pounds, with no deduction for food.

Should the full quota of *res* transport guaranteed by any village be already out on the road, then the traveller or merchant who arrives has to wait for its return, or else make his own private arrangements with any other transport he can find, at such rates as they choose to ask.

To anybody who likes to look back into the past, and trace the continuity of human things, it is an added charm to the Ladakh road to watch your slow-moving ponies and yaks, or your little black dzos, which are the hybrid offspring of yaks and cows, more docile, better able to support heat, but not so powerful as true yaks. You know that the roads you follow have been followed for centuries by travellers, and that a caravan of a thousand years ago would have moved in just the same way; the drovers would have worn the same clothes; would have loaded their bundles on to the same rough, wooden saddles, with the same coarse, black, hairy ropes as your modern tents are tied on with to-day; would have covered the same stages in the same time; would have made their wayside meals by the same little bubbling springs as you do now, and cooked their barley in the same shaped pots, and drunk their buttered tea from the same kind of little silver-lined bowls, carried in the bosoms of the same rough woollen gowns, as do your ponymen of to-day.

There is a soothing charm in the thought, as you lie in the shade of a rock or a tree, if it be summer, or bask in the sunlight in spring or autumn, to eat your midday meal on the road. Hilaire Belloc says that one of the great virtues of the Mass is that when you go to Mass in the morning—if you happen to be a Catholic—you are doing something which many men have done for many hundreds of years. For which reason also, he adds, all men should dig in a garden, should shoot at a mark, and should drink fermented liquor from time to time, because all these customs are age-old and, consequently, possess virtue. I would add to this excellent list that all men should from time to time take the wild roads, carrying their few possessions upon stunted little ponies and the other pack-animals of the wild places—the great, slow-moving yaks, the little pack-sheep, the donkeys and dzos, or the rough-coated camels—moving a stage a day, and sleeping out in the starlight; for these things also many men have done for many centuries, and there is a magic and a charm about the doing of them which dispel the over-hurried thoughts of an over-hurried civilization.

Life for the Ladakhi villager is a succession of days upon the road, alternated with days in his fields. He is of the earth, very earthy, much taken up with the matter of crops and animals, ignorant of books and movies, of wireless and politicians, of strikes and lock-outs, and the myriad other benefits conferred upon us by that Frankenstein monster—" progress."

Moreover, he is almost entirely self-supporting, save only for a few luxuries, which the West has thrust upon him, and for the tea which has come to him for centuries from China, and which can hardly be counted as a luxury, since it has become a staple of his frugal diet. Matches, and sometimes kerosene oil, safety-pins and English needles—these are his main luxuries, and these have to travel to him from the outer parts of the world.

For the rest, he draws on his own country. He has to clothe himself, since, æsthetic reasons apart, the cold demands clothing at the altitude at which he lives, and so he spins the wool of the local sheep and goats. Half the men and women you meet are spinning as they walk, spinning mechanically on a spindle from a hank of wool, almost the whole day long. Then the women will weave the spun yarn into narrow strips ot clcth on rough, home-made looms, and fashion the narrow strips into garments.

He must be shod, for the roads are rough, and therefore he shoes himself with rough, string shoes that he makes from his homespun yarn, and soles them for the road with home-cured hide—preferably pony-hide, cut from dead animals found on the roadside, half sun-tanned already, and hand-worked for days until it is sufficiently pliable to use. Except when he is actually on the road, or engaged in cooking his scanty food, the Ladakhi is always busy with some little job: making his string shoes; twisting a piece of pony-hide to make it into something like pliable leather; patching his rough clothes; sewing up his coarse bits of pack-harness with the big needles he carries on his belt.

Then there is butter to be made from the milk; there is grain to be ground, and a hundred other necessary tasks. In fact, he lives the kind of life that the Bolshevik and Communist would have us all live, and, in consequence, has no time for anything else, such as thought or invention or the amelioration of human conditions. If you have to do everything for yourself you will find the day is all too short, and life, as we know it, became possible only when someone with a brain in advance of his contemporaries realized that the economical way to live was to let one expert make everybody's boots; another expert do all the cooking; a third take on the bricklaying; a fourth manage the plumbing, or whatever they did in that line in the year 1,234,567,890 B.C. Then somebody, anyway, had a certain amount of spare time to think out such problems as how to make a sheep grow more wool, and somebody else was able to draw pictures or tell stories, and thus lay the foundations of the various arts which have contributed so much to make life more gay and less drab.

And, of course, as is inevitable if everybody does everything, nobody does anything well, so that the Ladakhi would, I think, take the booby prize for the superb inefficiency of everything he turns his hand to —which, nevertheless, does not prevent him being an extremely delightful person to handle and to march with, once you have shed your foolish Western conception as to time being money and, therefore, more important than anything else in the world.

I do not fancy anybody in Ladakh, not even the most erudite Skushok, understands time. Most Skushoks own a watch or a clock, but I honestly believe they are the only Ladakhis who do. The Santanling Skushok welcomed me, greatly hoping that I would mend his American alarm, which had stopped five years previously. The task was beyond my limited powers, but the news did not upset him very much—doubtless he trusted that in another five years or so some better-educated traveller would arrive, and the clock would begin to tick again, and so add an air of further mystery to the wonders of the Skushok's apartment as seen by his generally ignorant and always credulous visitors.

But the Ladakhi is fortunate in one thing, and that is, in his climate, which is bone-dry. In such a dry climate you can build houses that stand up in utter defiance of all the laws that apply in any other part of the world.

He builds himself a house of mud and stone, with a flat roof of peeled poplar-trunks, crossed with a layer of willow wands, supporting a flat roof of mud, and since it hardly ever rains it keeps over his head, year in, year out. It is a small house and, probably, windowless

—or, if there be a window, glassless, and it is generally closed by a wooden shutter to keep out the wind.

Interiorly it is dark—very dark—and the darkness is intensified by the fact that plastered walls and woodwork are alike covered with a thick coat of soot from butter-lamps and dung-fires, for wood is scarce, and, such as there is, is generally too valuable to burn, so that yak- or cow-dung instead is used as fuel.

The kitchen is, of course, the chief room, and sometimes it is well worth seeing. The central feature is the great blackened clay stove, at which presides the wife, with her copper-pots bubbling over the fire. Around the walls on rough shelves are arrayed her pots and pans, and these are generally well kept and bright. Hung in a corner will be the big, black, wooden churn for churning the butter-tea, and in another corner will be sacks of barley, unless, as happens in the bigger houses, the grain is kept in a sort of dry well, dug in a corner of the room, and covered with a flat stone.

At one end is a raised platform where the family eat, and where, incidentally, they sleep in the winter, and before this a low table on which are the teapots of hammered brass and copper—great big family teapots, made to stand over dishes of hot ashes.

The servant question has not, so far, arisen in Ladakh, for everybody has a servant—every woman, that is, save only the very poorest—a female servant, of course, who comes for a year or two in exchange for her keep and her clothes. She is probably a girl from one of the wilder, poorer valleys, who wants to see a little of the world, and perhaps gain something towards her marriage portion when she, in turn, will be able to take on a servant—"a fire blower," as the Ladakhi has it, for the servant's work is to light the fire, while the mistress of the house herself does the cooking.

No self-respecting Ladakhi woman would be without a servant on these lines, and even the woman-servant in a European house has her own servant to help with the little house where she lives when off duty, for, as a rule, they do not live in, as we expect servants to do elsewhere.

The Ladakhi woman does not wear a wedding ring, but, nevertheless, she has the outward signs which in all communities seem inevitable in some form or other to denote whether a woman is married or not. I do not know why such importance should be attached to displaying this fact among women, whereas in most races the bachelor and the husband are generally indistinguishable.

The unmarried Ladakhi woman braids the numerous plaits of her hair with white string, the married woman with black, and if your eyesight is keen you can usually contrive to distinguish the colour; there is generally some portion which still retains a semi-greyish hue that tells you the cords are, conventionally speaking, white.

The trousseau is a most important feature in Ladakhi life. There is a list of minimum requirements, which include, I think, six dresses, three pairs of trousers, a pair of ear-flaps, a pair of shell-bracelets, and the goatskin cape. But quite an average number of dresses for a girl is twenty, with everything else in proportion. What she does with them I cannot discover. I think she locks most of them up, and saves them for her daughter's wedding, because, however gaudy her *peragh* and her jewellery may be, her clothes always seem in the last degree of decrepitude. I think, however, this is partly due to the fact that the Ladakhi has never heard of the proverb, "A stitch in time saves nine." I think she puts on one dress and wears it until, after a few years, it falls to pieces, and then she starts another. You see she is not handicapped by the dictates of fashion, which is strange in a daughter of Eve.

Her clothes never vary, and she is not compelled to shorten and lengthen her skirts, nor to alter her figure to fit her clothes, as the Western woman is. Nor has she to ponder between the merits of shingle, bob, or Eton crop.

Moreover, she does not have to do her hair every morning; in fact, I think, to be accurate, she does it about once a year—after the harvest is over. The dust and dirt gathers up during the harvest months—standing out winnowing grain in the wind is a grimy proceeding—and at that time of year she very often discards her *peragh* and wears a small cap, like her Mussulman sisters, and then when harvest is over she does her annual hairdressing, a proceeding that takes some time.

As an almost invariable rule, the Mussulman Ladakhi women do not wear the *peragh*, sporting in its place a rather attractive little cap or veil, set with a gold ornament or a cluster of turquoise. The reason given for the campaign that the Mussulmans lead against the *peragh* is that very often a new turquoise, or the beginning of an extra row of the bright stones, indicates the successful conclusion of a love affair. Jealousy is not a failing of the Ladakhi man, but such of him as have been converted to Islam have picked up something of this predominantly Mussulman trait.

I think that all the trouble which woman elsewhere invariably takes over her clothes is in Ladakh devoted to her strange head-dress, and therefore she can neglect the rest of her apparel. The Christian or Mussulman women who have given up the *peragh* seem to take much more pains about the remainder of their toilet than do their Buddhist sisters. In Leh you notice a good deal more in the way of attractive, new-looking clothes than you do in the more purely Buddhist parts, and yet, I suppose, the cost of a new row of turquoises can be very little less than that of a dress of gaily printed cotton.

Harvest time in the villages, to my way of thinking, is one of the most attractive seasons of the year, chiefly because the Ladakhi is fond of music of all sorts, but more particularly of the flute and of singing. You are awakened at sunrise by music on all sides, and you look out, in the growing sunlight, to see the fields full of people cutting the crops or garnering the grain, stacking the long sheaves to dry in the sunlight, and singing the whole while—old, old songs of harvest-time, come down from the days when Ladakh was a free kingdom under its own rulers, an offshoot of the wilder country of Greater Tibet. But I do not suppose that life has changed very much, for all that it now forms part of Jammu and Kashmir, and so of the Indian Empire.

I expect that when Moorcraft—who was the first European to give us any real description of this quaint country, just over a hundred years ago—marched up into Ladakh he saw the same sights, and talked to the same kind of people, as you and I do to-day. At least, his book sounds as if he did, save only where he deals with the King and the Court of Leh.

And I think that it will be a very long time before it changes much. It is a hopeless country for a motor-car, even if anyone contrived to find a way for a car over the passes out of Kashmir. It is a worse country from the point of view of flying—a jagged tangle of peaks and mountain ranges, interspersed with narrow river valleys and terraced fields, where even a light fighting Scout would find it hard to come down without crashing.

There is, therefore, every hope that for centuries to come the Ladakhi village will remain what it is to-day, and what it has been for centuries—a more or less self-contained little community of people, entirely immersed in their orchards, their crops and their dwarf-cattle; making processions to scare away the demons who sometimes stop the glaciers from melting in the summer, and so stop the water-supply on which the villagers' little all depends; a land where people like you and me can still escape for a space from the motor and the telephone, from the parrot cry of "efficiency," which is the bane of modern life. I wonder Mr Gandhi did not go up to Ladakh; he would have found there nearly all that his heart craves, and each time I get to Ladakh I become more of a Gandhi-ite in my leanings to his utterly impracticable ideas of a world reformed. Dreams are generally impracticable things to pit against modern civilization, but nevertheless they are fascinating beyond everything, and of all the places I know I have never found any so friendly to dreams as the byways of Lamaland.

CHAPTER NINE

LEH

CHAPTER NINE

Leh

LADAKH is a country of villages—for the most part small hamlets—and, as a consequence, Leh stands out as a real town, though elsewhere it would be reckoned as but little more than a fair-sized village.

But, size apart, it has many features which mark it out from the villages of Ladakh. It possesses a bazaar, a genuine bazaar, with shops where you can buy almost anything you want—if, that is, your needs are comparatively simple. It has, moreover, a real palace—a tall, many-storeyed building, standing upon the hill which forms a background to the town—and though for most of the year the palace lies empty, still, in the New Year, the King of Ladakh comes there for a while, after making his semi-state entry. He has no real position, but the Ladakhi is conservative and the nonentity who resides on his own land at Stok, across the Indus, is the descendant of the only hereditary dynasty of Ladakh.

But its real claim to importance is, that it is the mart where the incoming trade from Central Asia meets the upcoming trade from India and the cross-current of the Tibetan trade. In August and September, Leh bazaar is packed with the merchants and drovers of half a continent, and the *serais* are filled with skull-capped, long-coated and long-booted merchants of Kashgaria, and with the pilgrims on their way to or from the Indian coast, whence sail the steamers to the Haj ports—the gates of Mecca and Medina—sacred places to the Mussulman.

Leh is, in a sense, a city set on a hill, and visible from far off. It lies in the valley running down from the Khardong hills to the Indus—a long, triangular-shaped valley, ever broadening as it nears the great "Lion's Mouth" River, as the old Ladakhis called the Indus, for, according to the Tibetan belief, the four great rivers they know each emerge from the mouth of some fabled beast. The valley slopes upwards at the rate of some hundred feet to each mile of stony, sandy going—a great fan, which Conway, I think, attributed to mud-avalanches in the past before Ladakh settled down to the state of physical equilibrium which marks it to-day, in striking contrast to Gilgit, where the mountains are still trying to find their balance, so to speak, being comparative children among the mountain ranges of the world.

It is strikingly visible as you approach it from the side of India, the more so for the fact that your last two stages have been over very desolate country—long expanses of sand and gravel, tiring to eye and leg

CHANREZIG. A life-sized image of the thousand armed GOD of Pity.
CHORTENS in which the ashes of the dead are placed. A feature of every Ladakhi Village.

alike. But suddenly at Spitok you turn sharp left, up a little gorge of clay cliffs, leaving to your right the half-ruined *chortens* leading up to Spitok *gompa*, mostly hidden from you by a spur of the hill on which it stands, and then, lo! before you, so close that you feel you have but to reach out a hand to touch it, stands Leh.

It is really five miles away, but in the thin, clear atmosphere of Ladakh it seems no distance at all, as you rein up your pony to look out at the big mass of green—green of fields, dense masses of poplar- and willow-trees; glimpses of white houses among the green; long lines of *chortens* and *mane* walls; and, above all this, the imposing square mass of the great palace on the Namgyal hill—the Tsemo, as the Leh people call it.

If it be spring, then the whole will be backed by the white snows of the Khardong hills, culminating in Nangasago's 19,000 ft., and slightly to the left of Leh you see the dip of the Khardong Pass, where runs the road to Central Asia. It is an imposing sight on a fine spring day, under a cloudless sky of vivid blue, and if you are a proper traveller it gives you quite a little thrill. The road is good, but so also are the big halting-places, and when you have been some three weeks on the march there is something thrilling about the first sight of a town, where you are going to halt a while, and where you will meet the people from the farther side—from the outer lands. But if it is spring you will not meet many of them yet awhile, only such as have sojourned in Leh for the winter, since the Khardong Pass is not yet open, and the second week of June is about the earliest date that one can hope for if one is going on into Nubra or beyond.

I crossed the Khardong this year with the first caravan, and the date was the 13th June. It was no child's play to force the pass, with its heavy covering of winter snow hiding the glaciers that dip over on the north side, and make the 17,400 ft. of the Khardong—just about 6000 ft. above the altitude of Leh—a difficult and tiring ascent, where the unladen ponies had to be man-handled over with ropes, and in the worst places pulled over the snow on tent-flies and *suleetash* spread out, to make a way, like the grass-matting tracks used in Palestine and Sinai during the war. In fact, our crossing had been made possible only by several days' hard work on the part of the advance party of the Mason Expedition—driving unladen yaks up to plough a way, and using men to cut and improve the track they made.

But the Khardong, though only eight miles or so from Leh, is a far stage yet when you ride up from Spitok to Leh, for you are certainly going to halt for several days, even if the pass is open. If you are going on, then Leh is the last place where you can refit—the last place where you can get any reasonable quantity of supplies—the last post and telegraph office—the end of the single wire you have followed these last two hundred and forty miles since you set out from Srinagar.

And therefore you approach it with some feeling of exhilaration at the thought of sitting still for a day or two, of eating your meals at reasonable hours, and of being able to take things out of boxes and keep them out, instead of having to replace them again the same evening, when they have only emerged at, perhaps, three o'clock in the afternoon.

At the end of the long, shelving plain, when you have come into the outlying fields and trees, you follow a narrow, stone-walled track and pass a wayside shrine containing three *chortens*—a very favourite type of building. Not real *chortens* these, since they are not primarily designed to hold the pork-pie relics of departed Ladakhis. These are miniature *chortens*, only a couple of feet high—three of them—each bearing a big Sanskrit letter painted in a different hue.

The trio of them stand in a three-walled shrine, open on the fourth, the inner walls being adorned with paintings and stencillings, in gaudy contrast to the spotless white *chortens*, whose only dash of colour is their red spirelets and the initial letters which tell you that they represent the Buddhist Trinity—Buddha, the Law, and the Church. And, perhaps, standing by the shrine you may see a Ladakhi woman, in her quaint clothes, with goatskin cape and basket upon her back, telling her rosary of one hundred and eight beads—on each of which, as it passes through her fingers, she will murmur the Buddhist formula: "Om mane padme hum." Or, maybe, you will see an old, goat-bearded man busily turning his brass prayer-wheel and, with his disengaged hand, spinning wool.

And then, turning up a wider lane, you are guided through a great gate into a long street—the bazaar of Leh—with houses on either side of you, shuttered and closed for the main part, since the trade has not yet begun to arrive, and these houses are mostly rented by the incoming merchants. On either hand stand tall, graceful poplars, the universal tree of High Asia, where there happen to be any trees at all, and before you, at the end of the long street, springs up the hill upon which stands the palace you saw from far off.

You follow the street to its farther end, where you find the post office and the more permanent shops, which are open all the year—a corner where there is always a small crowd of people; market-women, with baskets of vegetables or fruit; drovers of the road, looking idly about them, gaping at the unaccustomed sight of shops and a crowd. Then, passing the little booths, where you may buy such luxuries as matches and cheap cigarettes, cheap American or German lamps, cotton cloth, needles and thread, yes, even buttons, you turn to your left and, passing through a rather winding street, come out into the European quarter. Here are the little bungalows of the Moravian mission, and, at the farther end, the dak bungalow and the big garden and house of the British Joint Commissioner, who, with his confrère, the Wazir or Governor of Ladakh, an official of the Kashmir State, manages the treaty road to Central Asia.

The dak bungalow is a fair-sized one, but with a small garden, and not much room for tents. If you are lucky enough to be a friend of the Joint Commissioner you may get permission to pitch your camp in his spacious garden under the cotton-poplar trees—the nicest garden I know in Ladakh—green and shady, under the barren hills, and with a beautiful view of the snow-topped Zanskar range, on the farther side of the Indus, crowned by the 20,000 ft. of Mount Sacrifice's snowy peak. And then, when your tents are pitched, you will remark the immediate disappearance of every servant you own—caught by the lure of the bazaar and the shops.

You will not find Leh dull, even if the state of the higher passes keeps you there for several days, for there is much to see, even if you know Leh and have been there before.

There are several monasteries—small ones—of which

my own favourite is the yellow-cap *gompa* of Tsankar a mile or so from the dak bungalow, very clean and most attractive, with endless frescoes, done by a man who had the gift of imparting an individuality to each of the faces he painted, so that, although there are rows of pictured lamas and bodhisats, each one seems different and, still more, each one seems to be a portrait.

Then there are the two monasteries on the Tsemo hill with the big statues of Buddha—each of them two storeys high, so that on the upper storey you are on a level with the chest of the great figure, and look up into the impassive face; and on the lower floor, feeling a very pygmy, you stand at the feet and look upward into the shadows, high beyond which the faintly-seen countenance catches the light from the upper-storey windows as Maitreya—the Buddha to come—sits there meditating through the centuries.

On the flanks of the rocky Tsemo hill you may see the ruined walls which once girt the royal town of Leh—walls and watch-towers and a ruined gate—the remains of the once strong fortifications that ringed the hold of the Ladakh king before the Dogras came.

Then there is the palace to visit, massively built, and many storeys high, but void of furniture and ornamentation, save only for its little chapel and for a couple of rooms where Royalty spends one or two of the winter months, and you may stand in Royalty's place in the carved-wood balconies, and look down into the court-yard where the dances are held.

In the same courtyard, also, you may see piles of wood, stacked there for fuel for the big annual festival, when all the monasteries have to send in lamas to hold a service for the Maharajah of Kashmir—visible sign of who is the real ruler. The pill is sweetened by the lamas being fed at State expense during the two days of the ceremony. Not, perhaps, that it is in any way a very bitter one, for the Buddhist is not much concerned with self-determination. Power is an attribute of the supreme, regardless of who may wield it, and the Government is the Government no matter who the temporary ruler may happen to be.

From the upper storey or from the roof you look out over Leh town itself, a huddled cluster of little flat-roofed buildings, typically Eastern, save only for the long array of prayer-flags. Beyond the town lies a yellow expanse of sand and stone, leading down to the silver ribbon of the Indus, on whose farther side the valley slopes up once more, to lose itself in the formless blue of the hills beyond.

Then if you want exercise you may take your dogs out for a walk down the road towards Hemis.

On one side of that road stand countless *chortens* and *mane* walls—real *chortens*, for the disposal of ashes—and on the other lie rows and rows of little Mohammedan graves, for there are many Mohammedans in Leh. There is also one small building, the isolation hospital, which an unimaginative administrator of the past planted alongside the cemetery and *chortens*. I do not suppose he had studied modern medicine or heard of Napoleon's maxim anent the moral and the physical. However, the Ladakhi is not an imaginative person, and the fact of the view from his sick-bed being countless rows of tombs would probably not affect him as much as it might you or me.

If you are disposed to face a small hill you might go a little farther, and climb up the little rocky eminence where the Shushot road drops down into a narrow gorge, and visit the small chapel where lives the tutelary god of Leh, for just as each house has its special protector, so has each village its own god, and the only town owns a very special spirit.

And then in the pleasant, long, shadowed evening you may come back and watch the polo—the national game of Baltistan and, to a lesser degree, of Ladakh—played in a dusty side street, with no apparent rules or time, where the exponents of the game dash backwards and forwards, in a cloud of dust, on their little ponies. True maids-of-all-work, those ponies—carrying loads, carrying master, or playing polo to the strains of the local band—two drums and a clarinet—all contributing of their loudest and, therefore, of their best.

THE HEMIS DANCES. Entry of masked Buddhas attended by richly dressed Lamas.

HEMIS MONASTERY. The stage courtyard on a festival day. Lama dancers entering.

Then in the morning you may stroll about the bazaar and watch the types that collect there—Kashmiris, Ladakhis, men of Yarkand and Kashgar, of Turfan and Khotan, Tibetans of Lhassa, Chang Tang nomads, Indian moneylenders of the Shikarpur district—true sons of the horse-leech—and last, but by no means least, the regular soldiers of the Kashmir army, Gurkhas of the Bodyguard Regiment, which generally has a company stationed in Leh. As usual, they look upon themselves as foreigners in a strange land, greeting the European as a brother and a friend. Gurkhas always swagger, but I think those in Leh swagger more than they do elsewhere, as they saunter down the bazaar in their little glengarries, their black coats, and the gay sashes supporting their *kukris*—with roving eyes for such well-favoured damsels as may be seen.

Then there is also your own breed to be met—other travellers, shikaris, wanderers of all types, as well as the residents, whose hospitality is proverbial.

I knew a lady who lived many years in Leh, and she kept a visitors' book as a sort of souvenir of those who passed through. She showed it to me one day, and I read the names with interest, for she told me that many of the people who came to Leh were mad, but all were invariably interesting. Reading through the list of several years, I agreed with her in both counts.

That is also an added charm to your stay in Leh—

the wonder of whom you are going to meet: what new acquaintances you will make, what friends fortune may send you here; for it is always the most unlooked-for acquaintanceships that seem to happen in these less populous places.

And in these meetings there is something new, which you do not find in civilization—the camaraderie of the road which makes speech so far more free, and conversation so much more interesting. There is a feeling of freedom from convention; you are as ships that pass by, and so seem more free to be frank, to say what you really think; to put forth thoughts that elsewhere would never be voiced. Your roads have crossed for a moment in infinity; to-day or to-morrow you will part once more, probably never to meet again. And, illogically, somehow that leads to greater liberty of speech, though why this should be I know not. But it adds to the interest of life, because in ordinary intercourse half the world is busy using words to conceal its thoughts, whereas in Ladakh one uses speech to express one's ideas instead of to veil them.

And then, if you want to, you can waste your substance royally in buying curios—copper and brass teapots, relics from monasteries, little boxes for charms, or shrines for images, *dorjés* and bells, even painted *tankas*. Only I fear that Ladakh is becoming sophisticated in these matters, and that a regular trade is springing up in the making of such things, purely for sale to globe-trotters. Turquoises and semi-precious stones also may you buy—I think at a very much bigger price than you would pay for them in London.

Centuries ago a king of Ladakh set to work to reform the world by making everybody equal—taking from the rich to give to the poor. He carried out his plan three times running, though how he did it I do not know. The reason for doing it three times was, that human nature asserted itself again each time, and a few months after the rearrangement some had spent all they got and others had saved and added to their hoard. I do not know if his story is to be found in the Communist text-books which, I hear, are now handed out to youth in Europe. If not, it ought to be. The reason he could not do it a fourth time was that he died. But the idea has, I think, persisted subconsciously in the mind of the Ladakhi seller of curios, and he does his little bit to equalize things by taking from the rich, notably the American globe-trotters, and giving to the poor—himself.

Once upon a time it was considered good manners to do at Rome as the Romans did. My one complaint against the transatlantic tourist is that he or she will not fall in with this old maxim, and pays New York prices in Ladakh. This is disturbing to the countryside, and sometimes leads to real distress among the poorer people of the country, who actually go in want because there is rumour of the impending arrival of Americans, and the *banias* and shopkeepers hoard their goods in the hope of selling them at unheard-of prices to these God-sent lunatics, for so the Ladakhi looks upon the folk who appear not to understand the value of money.

This is a digression, for I was talking of Leh, where you may see many things, and many kinds of people of all races, and very often find that by no means the least interesting are those of your own colour. And you will find that a week, or even a fortnight, is all too short to take in the atmosphere of the place, which is a sort of microcosm of all Ladakh, showing you something, but not the whole, of all the different peoples whom you will meet on your wanderings if, as you and I are going to do, you go still farther afield.

CHAPTER
TEN

HISTORY

CHAPTER TEN

History

TRAVEL is a fascinating pursuit, even when it only implies the continual seeing of new lands, of strange mountains and rivers. But the greater part of the charm is lost if there are no people to see, or if one knows nothing about the customs and beliefs of such inhabitants as one may meet. In fact, it seems to me, the more you know about the people among whom you are going to wander the more pleasure will you derive from your travels. One ought therefore, I think, to start on one's journey with as much stored-up knowledge as may be found or assimilated. So only will you understand what you do see, and, what is still more important, be able to bring back something really interesting to weave into your description for less fortunate friends, to whom the chances of travel have been denied.

To understand any people at all you must have some knowledge, however slight, of their history, for the history of a people often explains much of what would otherwise be puzzling or incomprehensible—gives the key to their traits and qualities, to their customs and usages.

In a book like this one can, of course, give only the most sketchy account of the history of Ladakh, but even that, it seems to me, might be better than nothing, and in the same way as I have endeavoured to give little passing glimpses of the country and the people—of their habits, their ways of life, and their beliefs—so now I will attempt to recount some small portion of their history.

The population of Ladakh is made up of the three races I have already mentioned: the original Aryan Dards—the Brokpa, as the Ladakhis call them; the Mons, the early Buddhist people from Kashmir; and the Mongol stock from Tibet, who now form the majority of the inhabitants.

We know very little about the first two, whose history has been lost and overlaid by that of the newer arrivals, although even the history of these is far from complete.

Herodotus is probably referring to the Dards in his story of the gold-digging ants of the Indus Valley, the fabled ants who dug out the gold from the river sands —"ants smaller than dogs, but bigger than foxes." He mentions also how venturesome men would set out to get the gold, arriving during the heat of the day when the ants were underground, since only in this way could they hope to fill their saddle-bags and escape from the wrathful ants.

As in all old fables, there was a substratum of truth.

The men of the Indus Valley did dig for gold—do so still, though without great profit. And from a distance the burrows they make in the ground and the rough clothes they wear might, to a vivid imagination, conjure up the picture of gigantic ant-heaps. Pliny tells us that the country of the Dards was rich in gold, and so confirms, indirectly, the idea that it was the Dards in the Indus Valley of whom Herodotus wrote.

Of the Mons we know almost as little; they have been far more submerged than have the Dards, who in places still exist in complete colonies, whereas the Mons are now to be seen only as survivals in the lowest occupations, such as itinerant musicians, leather workers, and the like. But even to-day the old ruins which are to be found in the more remote valleys are spoken of as the "castles of the Mons," and the workmanship displayed in these buildings and rock-carvings points to a race far more highly developed than are their descendants of to-day.

Lastly came the nomad Mongol people from the East, and the resultant mixture of blood has produced the modern Ladakhi, whom you will find different in feature from the purer-blooded Mongols of the eastern district. Franke, the only modern historian of Ladakh, says that what we find pleasing in the features of the modern Ladakhi is due to the old Mons or Dard blood, and what displeases us comes from the Mongol strain. I take it he means æsthetically pleasing, for, personally, I often find a cheerful, slit-eyed Mongolian countenance much more to my taste than the Kashmiri or Dard, of far cleaner-cut features.

The Chinese pilgrim, Fa Hien, who came to India about A.D. 400, mentioned Ladakh, and it is interesting to note that the Chinese record speaks of two Tibets, Great and Little, from which the still-used term of "Little Tibet" is probably derived. Strange to say, the term was applied to Baltistan rather than to Ladakh, although to-day, if the term is used at all, it is applied to Ladakh, and politically is just as inadmissible as it would have been, prior to 1918, to speak of Alsace Lorraine as "Little France."

The Chinese records of those days speak of Ladakh as being entirely Buddhist, but the Buddhism of that time was subsequently submerged by the more debased form introduced from Tibet, to which, up till the tenth century, Ladakh was subject. In that century the Empire of Tibet broke up, and the outlying districts set up as independent states, Ladakh being ruled by Palgyi Gon, great-grandson of the Tibetan emperor, Langdarma, who is to Tibetan Buddhism what Julian the Apostate was to early Christianity.

From thenceforward Ladakh was merely nominally under the suzerainty of Tibet, much as Tibet has been under the shadowy protection of China.

The outermost portion of the old Tibetan Empire, Baltistan, became Mussulman about the same period, and much of the extinct history of Ladakh deals with the wars between it and Baltistan, culminating in the successful Balti invasions, in the early seventeenth century, under Ali Mir, Chief of Skardu. It is recorded that the Baltis, filled with fanatical zeal, burned the temples and monasteries, destroyed the images, and cast the libraries into the rivers, so that prior to this date no reliable records are to be found, save only the rock-cut inscriptions which Franke mentions.

Ali Mir, however, did not attempt to annex Ladakh, contenting himself with forcing the Ladakhi king, Jamyang, to marry his daughter, Gyal Katun, having first divorced his legitimate Ladakhi wife. The lamas appeased popular sentiment by declaring that Gyal Katun was a reincarnation of the White Tara, and Ali Mir embellished the story by recounting a dream which he had had, wherein he saw a lion leap from the river and enter the body of Gyal Katun. This was of course interpreted to mean that she would bear a very valiant son, which, indeed, she did, the Prince Sengge Namgyal, "The All-conquering Lion." Sengge Namgyal lived up to his high-sounding title, having probably inherited his Balti grandfather's soldierly qualities.

He dealt firmly with the subsequent ruler of Baltistan, who invaded Ladakh, defeating him with considerable loss at Shimsha Kharbu. He then turned his attention eastward, captured Rudok, and even planned a campaign against Lhassa itself, which, however, he did not actually carry out, although he collected the outlying districts of Purigh, Spiti, Zanskar, and some other minor territories.

Sengge's son was Deldan, who is noticeable for his piety and his zeal in building temples and monasteries, though not so noteworthy in this respect as his father, who, in the interludes of wars, had laid out a grandiose building campaign, much of which had to be finished by Deldan. Lastly, he defeated the Baltis again, and Baltistan came under Ladakh, so that the Ladakhi kingdom reached the zenith of its glory.

In the latter part of the seventeenth century the Tibetans invaded Ladakh and carried their success right down to Basgu, where the Ladakhi army held out, but was unable to drive back the Tibetans. Delegs, the then King of Ladakh, despairing of regaining his country, sought help from the Mogul Emperor of Delhi, who held, amongst other countries, Kashmir. The help was forthcoming on conditions, the chief of which was that Delegs should become a Mussulman and build a mosque in Leh, both of which things he did, changing his name to Akabat Mahmud Khan.

The lamas say he did not, but the balance of the evidence goes to prove that the Mohammedan historians are correct, and although, doubtless, Delegs reverted to his original faith after the Mogul troops left Ladakh, his son Jigpal, who went as a hostage to Kashmir, became a genuine Mohammedan, and seems not to have returned to Ladakh.

Thereafter, however, the Ladakhi king seems to have paid an annual tribute to the Governor of Kashmir, which had now, on the decay of the Mogul Empire, come into the hands of the Sikhs, and the most important factor in the future of Ladakh was that the Dogra Raja Dhyan Singh of Jammu was a personage of great power in the Sikh Durbar, and he was very determined that his elder brother, Raja Gulab Singh, should secure Ladakh.

The state of Jammu was then busy in a process of aggrandisement, and had annexed all the small hill-states between the Jhelum and the Ravi. Kashmir as yet belonged to the Sikhs, but Gulab Singh's most recent acquisition was Kishtiwar, and Kishtiwar touches Ladakh.

When Gulab Singh had consolidated Kishtiwar, he sent Wazir Zorawar Singh to invade Ladakh, and in August 1834 the Dogra forces entered Ladakh from the Suru Valley. They had a hard fight at the outset, but were eventually successful, and finally advanced to Pashkum, in the Wakkha Valley, on the main Kashmir-Ladakh road.

After a protracted period, the king, Tsepal, finding that he was unable to drive out the Dogras, came to terms at Basgu, and after an agreement had been concluded invited Zorawar to visit Leh, but without his army. This Zorawar did, thereby very nearly coming to grief, since at the Durbar, when he was making a ceremonial present to the king's son, the latter, thinking the act of swinging a bag of gold round his head to be either an insult or an impending attack, drew his sword.

King Tsepal went down on his knees, clasping Zorawar's feet in Oriental fashion, and bloodshed was averted; but Zorawar's army came into Leh forthwith; Ladakh was declared a vassal state of Jammu, made to pay an annual tribute of 20,000 rupees, and to find at once 50,000 rupees towards the cost of the war. When this last amount had been paid, partly in cash, partly in kind, Zorawar left Leh and marched back to Lamayuru.

The Sikhs were not at all content to see Ladakh as a feudatory state of Jammu, and the Sikh Governor of Kashmir proceeded to foment as much discontent as he could. The first-fruits of his intrigues were that the Ladakhi Chief of Sod raised a rebellion, marching against the small Dogra post in Suru, which he captured, and then, very unwisely, put the garrison to the sword.

Zorawar stands out among Oriental conquerors as a man of clemency, and hitherto he had been not only politic, but merciful, in his dealings with his enemies. But this outrage was too much, and when he had recaptured Suru he proceeded to hang all the Ladakhis in the place, which after all was merely justice, and then offered fifty rupees per Ladakhi head. The local inhabitants were keen to earn the rewards, and they brought in about two hundred supposed rebels, who were all duly beheaded.

The punishment had its effect, for the local chiefs came in at once and promised to behave in future, and the Zanskar people quickly followed suit.

It was only just in time, for Zorawar now got news that the King of Leh had joined the rebellion, closed the roads to merchants and, moreover, imprisoned and tortured the Dogra agent at Leh—Munshi Daya Ram.

Zorawar made a most remarkable march through the extremely difficult mountain country of Zanskar, emerging at the bridge-head of Shushot, only a few miles from Leh. King Tsepal, seeing that the game was up, hurried out to pay submission and apologize for what had happened.

Zorawar rather exceeded his powers here, because he deposed Tsepal, and put Moru Tadsi, Khaloon of Banka, on the throne, for which he was reproved by Gulab Singh. Zorawar thereupon said he was quite ready to replace Tsepal, and did so—his task being rendered easier and more equitable since Moru Tadsi had started a revolt on his own and laid siege to the small Dogra garrisons which Zorawar had left in Ladakh.

This time Zorawar dealt severely with such leaders as he could catch, and by dint of cutting off their hands and noses, removing their tongues, and the like, he was able to instil a reasonable amount of fear into the countryside, which saved in the end a good many lives on both sides, though he still had another rebellion to contend with in the cold weather of 1840-1841, when the Purigh people rose. However, Zorawar caught the leader, Sukamir, treated him in the usual fashion, and ordered his hand to be tied up on the Khalatse Bridge as a warning. This was the hand that was eaten by a cat, having been carelessly left lying about overnight by the dispatch rider. The good people of Khalatse got out of the implication of having stolen it only by hurriedly substituting another one, cut off the corpse of a lama who had died a few days before.

Zorawar then thought out a scheme for stopping these rebellions by making the Ladakhis join his army. He therefore decided to invade Baltistan and take the Ladakhi army with him. He had, moreover, the shadow of a flimsy pretext, since Ahmed Shah, ruler of Baltistan, had disinherited his eldest son, Muhammad Shah, and the prince had fled to Zorawar, asking for his help in the matter.

The Ladakhi army marched by a somewhat different

A Corner of Leh Showing the Palace.

In the foreground is one of the great Mane Walls.

route, and did no fighting until it met the Dogra forces at Skardu, which they had reached after a very gallant river-crossing over the frozen Indus. The joint forces were successful in taking Skardu, and Muhammad Shah was made ruler of Skardu in his father's place. Moreover, Zorawar Singh forced Ahmed Shah to give up two other leaders of the late Purigh revolt, and had them publicly mutilated. This long-armed justice practically finished the Ladakhi taste for revolt, and from thenceforward Ladakh was quiet.

Zorawar Singh was a notable soldier, and would have made his mark in a very much greater theatre of war. He was extremely brave, a good strategist and tactician, and, moreover, he was a politic leader. His treatment of the rebel chiefs may sound very barbarous, but it was quite in accordance with Oriental traditions. But in Zorawar's case it was reserved for the selected few, whereas elsewhere it would have been accorded to the many, and combined, also, with indiscriminate massacres.

True to his scheme of employing the newly conquered against outside enemies, so as to give them no time to plot against their overlords, he now projected a campaign against Tibet, laying claim to all those districts which in the past had formed part of the western kingdom of Ladakh, and took with him Balti and Ladakhi contingents, the Ladakhis being employed mostly on transport work.

He captured Hanle and Tashigang without much fighting, and plundered the monasteries, and during this advance, one, Ghulam, a Ladakhi Mohammedan of Shushot, distinguished himself as an iconoclast, boasting that he had cleared Spiti of idols. Eventually when Zorawar's advance guard—it was a Ladakhi corps—did meet the Tibetan army, it was utterly beaten and most of it killed. Ghulam Khan, unfortunately for himself, was not killed but taken prisoner, and subsequently tortured to death, partly with hot irons, partly by having small portions of his body cut off a bit at a time. The Tibetans did not mind being killed by the invaders; they did not mind being looted or having their houses destroyed; but they could not stand having their images broken up. Ghulam's fate stands out in comparison with that of the remaining prisoners, who were more or less well treated, and, according to the chroniclers, even provided with wives, while in captivity in Lhassa.

Zorawar, who, so far, had been very successful in his winter campaigns, had made a bad mistake in invading Tibet at this season of the year. His Baltis and his Dogras were unaccustomed to the climate of Tibet, and he was trying to fight at 15,000 ft. above sea-level in December. There is no wood there, and the *burtsa* is a poor fuel to keep warmth in human bodies. Some of his men even burned their gun-stocks, and many lost hands and feet from frost-bite.

His army was, therefore, in poor condition when, on the 12th December, the Tibetans finally assaulted his entrenched camp. Zorawar himself was wounded by a bullet in the shoulder and unhorsed, and though he tried to put up a fight with his sword, left-handed, he was killed by a spearman, and his army broke and fled. The resultant flight was a small edition of the Retreat from Moscow, and only about a thousand men got back to Leh.

The Ladakhis made one more effort at revolt on hearing of Zorawar's fate, and tried to regain their independence under the nominal leadership of their boy-king, Jigsmed Namgyal. The rebellion was only partial, but was assisted by detachments of the Tibetan army.

However, a well-equipped Dogra force was sent up, and the Ladakhi rebels and their Tibetan allies, fleeing from Leh, established themselves in a fortified camp at Drangtse. The Dogras turned them out by damming up the valley, and so flooding the Tibetan camp, and, once outside of their defences, the Tibetans were no match for the Dogras.

A peace was then concluded with the Tibetans, and Jigsmed Namgyal was deposed, the Dogra Raja of Jammu taking the place of the Ladakhi king, whose grandson is now a gelong in the monastery of Hemis. Jigsmed Namgyal was allowed to retain his hereditary estate of Stok, where the family still live, in very reduced circumstances, however, compared with the Royal state they once held.

Since then the history of Ladakh has been the uneventful history of a province of the consolidated state of Jammu and Kashmir, for, with the downfall of the Sikh power, Gulab Singh of Jammu, who had become our ally against the Sikhs, was given possession of Kashmir, and his troops aided us during the Mutiny, some of them being with the besieging force at Delhi in 1857. The Kashmir State forces—to give them the new title which has replaced the older and better-known one of "Imperial Service Troops"—have since then shared in a good many campaigns with the army of India, both on the frontier and overseas. But there have been no further Ladakhi contingents, such as Zorawar improvised for his last two campaigns.

The future of Ladakh, therefore, is now definitely bound up with the future of Jammu and Kashmir, and so with that of the Indian Empire, and its history, if somewhat more progressive than in the past, will, one hopes, be considerably less eventful than it was in the two centuries preceding the disappearance of the Ladakh dynasty of Sengge Namgyal and his successors.

It is not unlikely, judging by Srinagar rumours, however, that Ladakh will before very long once again see a ruler in person, for no ruler of Jammu has ever visited that northern corner of his dominions. The energetic new ruler of Jammu and Kashmir, Maharajah Sir Hari Singh, is reported to intend visiting the whole of his country, when occasion offers, to get first-hand knowledge for himself of the provinces which he intends really to rule. Being a keen horseman, the long ride up to Leh is not likely to deter him, and so, after nearly a century, the Ladakhi will have once more the prospect of seeing his ruler face to face. And that in all Oriental countries is considered fortunate, as those who attended the Delhi Durbar of King George will remember, since Their Majesties took their place in the old balcony of the Mogul Emperors so that the people might have an opportunity of looking upon their Emperor, who, to Indian ideas—even now, in spite of much seditionist propaganda—is still held by the mass of the people to be, what Akbar embodied in his title, "Zill'ullah," "The Shadow of God."

CHAPTER ELEVEN

HEMIS

CHAPTER ELEVEN

Hemis

FOR many of the people who visit Ladakh in the early summer their chief recollection is that of the devil-dances, and should you mention to them you also have been in Ladakh they will assume that you have been to Hemis to see the annual fair and mystery play. As a matter of fact, there are two such plays, large-scale ones, besides numerous small representations at the lesser monasteries. But since the big Spitok one takes place in the winter very few Europeans have the opportunity of seeing it, and therefore the mention of devil-dances conjures up for most of us a picture of Hemis, and of the road thereto.

Hemis is the largest red monastery in Ladakh, and lies some twenty-four miles east of Leh, up a gorge leading south from the Indus Valley—a sheltered position, which saved it from spoliation by the Dogras in Zorawar Singh's days. There was also a further factor which helped the monastery, in that the Skushok of those days lent his support to the invaders, so that Hemis became, or rather remained, the richest monastery in the country.

Should you chance to be in Leh in early June, with a few days to spare, as happened to me this year, your time will be well spent in visiting the festival, which has no fixed date, according to our calendar, but is dependent upon the full moon of the Tibetan month. The Tibetan calendar consists of a series of cycles of sixty years, each year being designated by a combination of one of the five elements: fire, water, earth, iron and wood; and of one of twelve animals. Thus, the first year of the cycle is the "Wood Mouse" year, the thirteenth is the "Fire Mouse" year, the fifth is the "Earth Dragon," the forty-fourth is the "Fire Sheep" year, and so on. The months into which the year is divided are known also by the names of the animals. At the expiration of each cycle of sixty years a new one is begun, using the same system.

The big Hemis festival is thronged with people from the Indus Valley, from Leh, and from the outlying districts, and Leh business seems to come to a very definite standstill. The one postman of Leh, a pigtailed Ladakhi of very Mongolian aspect, who owns a smattering of Hindustani and enough knowledge of English script to deliver your letters, may be found there, from which I imagine there are no postal deliveries in Leh during the two days of the Hemis play. The postman probably goes there as a fellow-craftsman, for he is an amateur actor of some renown, and may always be seen performing in the various entertainments which the Leh officials give during the summer.

There is a distinct air of holiday when you take the road for Hemis for the play. For several days previously you will have noticed new and strange types congregating in Leh bazaar, as they pass through on their way to Hemis. If you have Ladakhi servants you will find your following has increased considerably overnight, and, on inquiring who the new-comers may be, you will find that they are nephews and cousins, or perhaps only friends, who propose to make the journey in your shadow, and so secure better camping accommodation and better seats at the spectacle.

You drop out of Leh through the Vallée des Tombeaux, down through the little gorge, and, following a stony, sandy track, flanked with great *mane* walls and *chortens*, come in time to the Shushot Bridge, in a wider portion of the Indus Valley sown with little villages.

Once across the river you will begin to run into the main stream of the people who are gathering towards Hemis, group after group of laughing, chattering folk —whole families with children, and with the very babies carried in the conical baskets on the women's backs. Elsewhere you will pass a lady of higher status, in her best holiday clothes, with gay worked shawl instead of the usual goatskin cape with the rough hair worn inward, followed by three or four of her handmaidens, each with her basket, carrying food and comforts for their stay at Hemis. Elsewhere again a cluster of lamas from some outlying monastery, coming in to see the show with the air of brother-professionals on a busman's holiday. Then, again, a sleek, well-fed Leh merchant, coming out to Hemis to set up the little booth where he will peddle matches and cigarettes; tinsel ornaments and farthing mirrors; dried apricots and walnuts and other delicacies; which he will trade against the fine sheep's down, known as "Pashmina," brought in by the Chang Tang nomads from the East, doubtless swindling them outrageously.

People talk a lot of the colourful East; and, to my taste, one of the most colourful scenes is that of a Ladakh road on a festival day. The country itself is a riot of vivid colour, utterly different from the softer colours of tree-clothed landscapes. A sky of the most intense blue, above the naked hills of limestone and sandstone, with a sun that paints them every colour of the rainbow at different hours of the day—red and orange, yellow and brown, madder and blue, indigo and slate, mauve and lavender. And before you always the dazzling expanse of sand and stones, dotted with the poplar-fringed villages and gardens, and barred by the long, gleaming ribbon of the Indus, pouring down from Greater Tibet, heavy with the melting snow-water of the high hills.

And all along the white thread of the road are groups of foot-passengers in the gaudiest clothes—plum and warm browns, scarlet and turquoise of women's *peraghs*, embroidered shawls of reds and greens, glint of brass and silver and, sometimes, gold ornaments; little ponies, with high-peaked saddles, worked in ivory and metal. Then where you pass an irrigation channel, or a grove of poplars, are little groups sitting to their mid-day meal—a holiday picnic one this, as opposed to the ordinary meal of the roadside, with nothing to look forward to.

All the East loves a *tamasha*, but I think Ladakh loves one even more, perhaps because there are so few in the life of the ordinary Ladakhi.

And so at last, in the afternoon, if you have secured good ponies and been able to go through in the day, you will turn up the narrow rock gorge, marked only by a few *chortens* and *manes*, and a red-painted *hlato*, and so presently come in sight of the Hemis *gompa*, a tall building under a cliff, surrounded by a cluster of smaller dwellings; a five-storeyed block, whose roof is surmounted by the folded umbrella-like erections and the streamers of yaks' tails which are the signs of a monastery.

Here the crowd will be getting dense as you begin to pass through the little camps, where the sightseers have settled down—camps in name only, since but few of them have any form of tent. A camp means merely the spot where they have dumped their possessions and set up a fireplace, where one of the women is busy making tea in a great copper pot.

Farther on you pass the willow-plantation where the distillers and sellers of *chang* have congregated, within easy walk from the *gompa*, so that the audience can quench their thirst during the intervals between the dances.

And then, in the shadow of the *gompa* walls, you pass through a hilly space, filled with little booths, where you see the bareheaded, ragged Chantani women gaping at the wonders displayed—the little, celluloid-backed mirrors that, wonder of wonders, show you what your face is like; the gaudy boxes of matches; the tinsel necklaces and bangles; grain and fruit and tea and cigarettes; the booths of the turquoise-sellers—all alike housed in rough tents, worn-out canvas of India, or black yak-hair of the high plateaux.

The Hemis *gompa* likes to see lots of visitors, the more the better, since each is expected to make an offering—only just, after all, considering that seats are free. If you are known or have written to the Skushok you will be provided with a neatly labelled camp site, or if you are a personage of importance in the land, or have come with letters of introduction from the mighty, you will be housed in one of the monastery guest-gardens, where there will be a painted and carved pavilion in which you may live, if so disposed, or else use as a living- and feeding-room, and sleep in your tent. You will then, moreover, have a wall around you to keep off the curious, which, if you happen to be a woman, is doubtless an advantage, since the Ladakhi lady has her full share of feminine curiosity, and finds the strange ways of her white sister full of unceasing interest—almost, if not quite, as good as the quaint dances that will take place on the morrow.

If you have not sent word, and have not made friends of the mammon of iniquity, you will have to find a site yourself, not an easy task in the cramped valley, where every inch is taken up by the crowd. But a resplendent personage — the lay steward of the monastery — can generally arrange something for you, for one of his duties is to look after the comfort of visitors. He will also send word to you when the play is about to begin, because Ladakh is guiltless of clocks, and the mere mention of hours means nothing at all.

If you are wise you will make a preliminary reconnaissance of the theatre that evening, following up a steep and not over-clean lane into the lower storey of the monastery, where you pass behind the kitchen, with the big cauldrons that hold tea for fifty monks apiece—and that means a lot—along a dark passage or two, whose sides are fitted with prayer-wheels, so that you can gain merit, as you enter, by spinning them duly clockwise, and so come out into the big courtyard, whose central feature is two high masts, one covered with prayer-flags and the other with streamers.

You will certainly find a crowd here, for there is pretty sure to be a rehearsal—an undress one—in progress, and the crowd will be gathered on the flat roofs of the lower building and in the courtyard itself, around the walls, kept off from the actual "stage" area by a low, light trellis-work, and by the sallies and whips of two lamas, whose efforts are always rewarded by huge bursts of mirth on the part of the good-humoured crowd. There is an etiquette in the police work, since the whips are supposed to be applied only to the goatskin capes of the erring damsels who try to make short-cuts across the stage—on their way to greet acquaintances spotted in the crowd opposite. It is not considered fair to apply it to the lady's muscular calves as she scuttles out of reach.

There is no etiquette for men; the whip may be applied impartially, and, moreover, the offender's cap may be seized and the needles and pins in it confiscated. Needles and pins are valued possessions in Ladakh, and the owner generally sticks them in his cap, so that the lamas are able to lay in a good store this way.

At the moment the lamas are clad in their conventional robes of dirty, faded red—the actors are all lamas, the orchestra also lamas, and the traffic-control police likewise belong to the priesthood. But to-morrow the dancers will be clothed in Chinese silks and brocades, their features hidden in wonderful and terrifying masks;

THE BOY SKUSHOK OF SPITOK with his Gelong tutor and an attendant Lama.

A GROUP OF RED LAMAS with two novices, in the frescoed verandah of their Monastery.

the orchestra will be arrayed in their best priestly robes, with silk scarves, and the policemen will wear huge flesh-coloured masks, with yellow shirts and yellow tam-o'-shanters. I think they must have got hold of an old picture of the Bombay policemen when they designed that dress.

To-day the only signs of the festival garb of to-morrow are the big silk banners which are being hung out from the upper storeys—twenty-foot banners, adorned with a painting, on a heroic scale, of some sainted lama, perhaps Padma Sambhava, founder of the red sect, he who introduced Buddhism from India into Tibet.

The "dress circle," reserved for distinguished visitors, is a verandah above the orchestra—so perhaps one should more properly refer to it as the "stalls." There will be gathered the Leh officials, the European visitors, the Gurkha soldiery.

The "boxes" are opposite, being the gallery verandahs of the rooms in the main building, the biggest of which is the Skushok's preserve. They are empty now, but to-morrow will be filled with the monastery dignitaries and their friends—richly garbed gelongs of other *gompas*, ladies in flaunting headdresses of nine and ten rows of turquoises, small children in holiday attire.

Then you can return to your camp and, if you have been able to steal a copy, read some book on the Lamaism of Tibet until dinner-time, and try to get an idea of what the play will be about, for there is nothing else to guide you. There is no spoken part, and the low Ladakhi chants will not help, nor is there a programme or a book of the words.

You will get a rather mixed impression of what you are going to see, and glean the idea that it is really what in Old England used to be called a mystery play—that is, an attempt to give religious instruction under the guise of a theatrical performance. The scenes will depict to you something of the story of Langdarma, who was King of Tibet in the early days of Buddhism, and was a strong supporter of the old black-hat worship, which was mostly sorcery. He was strongly anti-Buddhist, and made things very unpleasant for the red lamas—the yellow sect had not yet come into existence.

However, he duly came to a bad end, being slain by a red lama, who disguised himself with a black coat lined with white, and a white pony painted black. He got into the Royal presence on the pretext of showing off a special dance he had invented, and when the king, being interested, came closer to him, the lama drew a concealed bow from his wide, loose sleeve, fitted arrow to string, and shot Langdarma through the heart. He then fled, turned his cloak inside out, rode his pony through the river so that the paint was washed off and, while the country was being scoured for a black-clothed man on a black mount, a white-cloaked man on a dirty-white pony rode quietly and peaceably back to his little monastery, and, in course of time, Buddhism flourished again.

Most of the play deals with Langdarma's adventures after death, and thereby serves the purpose of teaching the people what to expect if they have not been good. It also teaches the virtuous what kind of beings they will meet, and shows them the wiles of the demons who will seek to lead the disembodied spirits astray when they are wandering in space, seeking a new tenement. Incidentally, we shall see the final fate of Langdarma when he is handed over to the stag-headed god of hell.

Whether the people, or even the lamas, understand what is being acted is another matter. Much of it is customary ritual, dating back into the far past, and the betting is against the majority of them being able to give you any coherent explanation of what is taking place. But it is a *tamasha*, and actors and audience alike enjoy it to the full.

Then after dinner you may sit in your tent and watch the moon swing up above the great black hills that ring you round, lighting up the white spires of the *chortens*, casting her silver upon the tall white monastery building, with its string-courses of red-and-black-painted wood, and listen to the evening music—probably the same instruments and the same airs that were played when Moorcraft was in Ladakh, the same evening symphonies that King Sengge Namgyal must have listened to when he passed Hemis on his way to his Eastern campaigns in the days of the first English Charles, perhaps even older still than any of these.

To our Western ears it is strange music, because, like all Eastern music, it is built up of quarter-tones, to which we are not accustomed, which, in fact, I think only very few Europeans can recognize at all. But it is haunting, none the less, as you sit there in the moonlight and the shadows, listening to the call of the great trumpets and the faint shrilling note of the clarinets, with the drums forming a muffled undertone. It begins ever so softly, the wail of the clarinets sighing over the valley, caught by the whispering breeze, that is gently moving the leaves of the willows about you, all ghostly in the moonlight; louder now as the wind drops; softer again as it rises anew; then swelling up more strongly, until you hear the first long drone of the copper trumpets, that rises and falls, rises and falls, and then booms out grandly, as the drums, hitherto barely heard at all, roll up like distant thunder.

Then still silence for a space, till once again the sob of the reeds pours out from the roof of the dimly seen white building yonder above the huddled shadows of buildings and trees, where little yellow sparks show the last remains of the evening cooking-fires.

And so it goes on for perhaps a couple of hours—

strangely fascinating, strangely soothing, softened by the distance, mellowed by the wind. You will hear the drums, the trumpets, the clarinets, to-morrow, close by; all day will the music continue for the dances, but never with the same charm as it seems able to lend to the moonlit night. The most impressively religious thing I know in the Ladakhi monasteries is the evening music, and that of Hemis the most impressively religious of all.

Then when the silence of night comes down you will sleep, feeling somehow that you have really in your travels come into something pleasantly mysterious, and wake again to bright, long-shadowed dawn-sunlight in a normal world once more, with people moving about everywhere, the scent of wood-smoke and dung-fires, the chatter of voices and the movement of men and animals. But even when you are breakfasting off Mr Heinz's tinned delicacies—because for you also it is a day of holiday which demands something extra in the way of food—you will still have somewhere at the back of your mind faint remnants of the unforgettable charm of the night before.

Even when you go up among the laughing, chattering crowd hurrying into the monastery to take up their places, or to visit the chapels and bow their heads before the statues, or to make their offerings to the Skushok, or to the old King of Ladakh, who now lives the religious life in seclusion at Hemis—an old man, with the most priestly head I have ever seen among the many lamas I have met—to make the offerings of copper or silver, in exchange for which they will receive little strips of blessed cloth to fasten in cap or robe; even though you may become aware of dirt and tawdriness, may see revealed in the blazing sunlight the cracks and gaps and the shortcomings, you will still, I think, if you be understanding, be able to retain some of the glamour which last night's music cast over the scene.

You will feel that everything cannot be translated into terms of earth or of dirt or of matter; that there is something beyond, which all of us seek; something after which we grope; something which even the people of Ladakh, in their dim-sighted fashion, seek century after century; something transcending all we know—all we *can* know with these limited senses of ours, which for the moment are our only avenues of knowledge.

CHAPTER TWELVE

THE HEMIS PLAY

CHAPTER TWELVE

The Hemis Play

THE courtyard will be far more crowded to-day, and if, before taking our places in the visitors' gallery, we climb up the rickety ladder to the roof above, thronged with men and women, we shall see that all the neighbouring roofs are crowded in the same way, and that three sides of the courtyard are packed with onlookers, men and women of Central Ladakh and, mingled with them, nomads of the Chang Tang, heavily built men, with dull, hairless faces, generally bareheaded, and wearing the long Tibetan boots instead of the Ladakhi shoes. Their women, too, are often bareheaded, though here and there you may see the more graceful headdress of Greater Tibet—a hoop of scarlet, framing the wearer's head, and carrying a single row of turquoises, and without the rather grotesque astrakhan ear-flaps.

When the Skushok has made his State entry and taken his place on the throne, to the left of the orchestra, surrounded by incense-bearers, and lamas carrying lights and vases of holy water, the orchestra will commence, and the first dance takes place, a slow and stately pageant by lamas, in the old black-hat dress—the last outward relic of the Bon religion that Buddhism displaced.

It is a Dance of Purification, and each strange-clothed dancer carries a little branch of the holy *shukpa* tree with which to sweep the floor as he pirouettes round, curtsying and sweeping at intervals, and sprinkling holy water from the vessel in his other hand. The great black hats, with the drooping streamers, almost conceal the wearer's features, which, however, are unmasked, and the impression is somewhat that of conventional Chinese mandarins as one watches the slow-moving figures in the brocaded robes, the silk veils streaming from the wide-brimmed hats, as they turn slowly round, and the great skull ornaments, at the back and front of the waistband, catching the light.

Sometimes the orchestra is playing on the clarinets or the little drums; sometimes the big trumpets boom out; sometimes again the music is hushed, and replaced by rather sweet, monotonous chanting. Each musician has before him a low table, on which lie the long sheets of music, printed in a similar way to that of the books in the libraries—long sheaves of paper tied in bundles.

Later comes an entry of mixed dancers—wild human, semi-human, and demoniacal figures—many of which will appear later in separate dances. The dance is generally a circular one, clockwise round the courtyard, and very slow in pace; a regular Merlin dance of "mystic paces and waving hands," and always finishes in the same way. The dancers depart at regular intervals, generally in pairs, disappearing up the great flight of steps leading into the monastery building, through the way cleared for them among the groups of lamas who cluster on the stairway; past the temporary altar built up on the left, a draped table, carrying lights and bowls of offerings.

The policemen, in all their glory of grotesque flesh-coloured masks, yellow tam-o'-shanters, yellow shirts, and embroidered kilts above their bare legs, are busy shepherding late-comers off the stage with their whips, lolling on the barricades in quiet intervals, chaffing and joking with the crowd—probably in Rabelaisian terms, to judge from the sallies of laughter. During the actual dances, however, the crowd is quiet, and there is little laughter, though whether this is due to awe or to reverence I cannot say.

Then comes the entry of Buddha, represented by nine masked figures, showing forth the nine principal earthly lives of the great Teacher. It is a very ceremonial entrance, and the orchestra rises up as the figures troop down the steps, all masked and gorgeously robed, led by an early blue-headed incarnation, akin to those in many of the paintings and images one sees in the monasteries. Others follow, getting more and more like the figure we associate with Gautama, until at last, to slow music and chanting, under a baldachino supported by lamas, surrounded by mitred acolytes and censer-bearers, enters a slow-moving, rich-robed figure whose face, or rather whose mask, is unmistakably that of Sakya Muni.

Many travellers have remarked upon the similarity between Lamaism and Catholic ritual, and if one judges by external signs alone their remark is correct, for here also are the lights and flowers, here also are the censers and the mitres and the priestly robes, and those of the attendants on Buddha's entry are particularly gorgeous. Here also is the offering of bread and wine, represented by the fermented *chang* and the barley-meal, which is blessed and eaten, or flung to the four corners of the courtyard.

It is strange that between two religions whose moral tones, as evinced in actual practice by their respective adherents, are such worlds apart, one should find such close resemblances of external details. There is one thing, of course, to remember, and that is, that both are very old, and both understand the value of symbolism to mankind—the symbolism, for instance, that is such an integral portion of Masonry; the symbolism which it was left to the religions whose birth, comparatively speaking, is only of to-day and yesterday to discard.

Mankind has an innate belief in symbolism, the use of form and ceremonies as a means of directing thoughts to that which must lie behind, and Lamaism has this much in its favour, that it can turn anything and everything to the use of religion—that it calls nothing, *in se*, bad or unfit to use in worship of the Power who made all things. It is only the very modern world that can take its cue from Mohammed and label wine, for instance, as something inherently evil instead of taking the older, more logical, view that nothing whatsoever has even the power to be bad; that evil can exist only in one place, in man's mind—in that which distinguishes him from all the rest of creation—and in the use he may make of that creation which, for some reason, has been placed at his disposal.

To the undiscerning, to those whose vision is limited to what they can photograph and measure, I concede fully that in the Lamaist ceremonials, and in much of their ritual, there is vast resemblance to those of the Church of Rome, and I can well believe the local story which accounts for the failure of the Catholic mission in Leh by saying that the Ladakhi could see no great difference between his religion and this newly imported one. The Ladakhi is essentially a material person, even more so than many of the globe-trotters who come here, and are there not lights and flowers, pictures and rosaries and images, abbots and monks and nuns, in both? *Ergo*, they are obviously the same throughout. I and my dog both possess mouths and teeth—though I admit his are better than mine—consume food, propagate our kind in the same fashion, suffer in the same way, and sleep when we are weary. *Ergo*, we are almost indistinguishable, and my motives and his obviously identical. The logic seems faultless.

The entrance of the Buddhas is not so much a dance as a procession, and, after circling the courtyard, the nine figures take their seats below the gallery to the right of the orchestra; the main character, Siddartha Gautama, as he was known on earth, in the centre. Then, as the acolytes and incense-bearers withdraw, smaller masked figures, novices these for the most part, clothed in silk robes, come out and pay homage, representing celestial spirits bowing down before the saviour of the world.

And so the play goes on, slowly, with long intervals when the crowd may withdraw to the booths without, and vary their day by visiting the merchants' stalls, or sampling the *chang*-sellers' wares in the willow-garden.

When the Buddhas have withdrawn again, once more, in solemn procession, with blare of trumpets and wail of clarinet, another dance takes place; more quaintly garbed figures swarm out on to the stage, a strange medley now, showing men and demons of all ages and types—the ingenuity of the mask-makers is unceasing; old, withered men, in strange brazen hats; painted, pale-faced savages, such as the Romans of Rome may have conceived the Picts of the British border; blue-masked demons, whose bulbous heads are surmounted by tiaras of little human skulls; figures festooned with realistic coils of "innards," brandishing spears and tridents, and ghost daggers.

They dance in the same mystic circle the same slow stately paces, and vanish, to be replaced by a troupe of demons whose masks are further embellished above the skull-crowns with quaint, triangular flags, and each of whom carries a drum of the warming-pan pattern. These dance a different dance, forming in two parties, drawn up in line, facing each other, advancing and retreating with low drumming, that suddenly swells up and becomes furiously rapid, and then dies away again as, in time to the leader of each party, they wheel and retreat, wheel again and advance, until at last, breaking suddenly into wild eldritch shrieking, they flee, *en masse*, up the staircase in a kaleidoscopic vision of streaming panther-skins and half-seen demoniac masks.

Then you see the spirits they have been endeavouring to frighten, clothed in rags and tatters, symbolic of cold and nakedness, with drawn, white features; the disembodied souls flitting between the worlds, bereft of guidance, harassed by enemies, who dance in bewildered fashion, dashing now here, now there, leaping forward, and recoiling again before some new half-seen, perhaps half-imagined peril. The crowd is somewhat silent here. Maybe they are concerned with whether they have made offering enough to the lamas, or whether the figures before them are images of their own fate when they shall leave their present bodies and go forth into the void, with none to help, no well-fee'd lama to mumble prayers on their behalf.

Come then still more imposing figures—the stag-headed god of hell and his satellite deities, in their dog-toothed masks, skull-crowned and entrail-festooned, symbols of the fate they mete out to those who have led unworthy lives and, above all, neglected that primary duty of the layman in Lamaism—the support of his clergy. They dance, or rather pirouette, round the stage, with slow gait and a step that seems unchangeable—a long pace, balancing from one foot to the other, followed by a pause, and a slow circle on the foot just placed upon the ground; pause, advance, circle; and repeat.

Then high on the roof above us two red-clothed, mitred figures will appear, and play upon the conch-shells long blasts of sound, and, presently, we shall leave the emptying theatre, and go out with the crowd, watch the audience making its midday meal in the little encampments, thronging among the booths for their fairings. It is a laughing, happy crowd, with no aversion to strangers like you and me, save only that when we try to photograph some particularly well-dressed or well-favoured damsel she will laugh and, at the last moment,

GHOULS DEVOURING LANGDARMA'S CORPSE. The last scene of the great Mystery Play.

THE SHUSHOK'S THRONE BEFORE THE MAIN ALTAR OF A YELLOW CAP MONASTERY. In the centre is an image of Buddha and to the right a statue of Tsong Kaka, founder of the Yellow Order.

slip behind a companion or nudge some wrinkled grandam between her and the camera, and we shall have to begin the stalk again, to the joyous laughter of the onlookers. The Ladakhi has a strong sense of primitive humour, of the kind that used to be such a feature of the halfpenny comic papers — laughter at somebody else's discomfiture. To see some unfortunate take a toss off a pony, for instance, or get kicked by a yak, is productive of loud and sustained merriment, in which the victim, unless he be really hurt, invariably joins. However, being wise to Ladakhi customs, I now own a telephoto lens and, moreover, a pair of cameras, and when I have laid my bait I turn round and, ostentatiously, get to work with the second camera. The crowd edge up behind; those in front draw away, with grins, and I have but to turn and let off the already laid battery on those behind me. They roar with laughter at having been caught out, for the Ladakhi can always see a joke against himself.

Presently the red-mitred figures appear again on the roof, the conch-shell trumpets blare out once more, and the crowd troop slowly back—no unseemly hurry—no undignified tying to time, and after a while the dances begin anew.

The play lasts for two days, and the order of the dances varies, and varies moreover, I believe, from year to year. The next one we see may be what, for lack of a better name, I call the "Turk" dance, a fascinating scene, in which men in old Mongol warrior costume dance slowly round with brandished swords. It is rather striking, for they wear old costumes and weapons that make one think of pictures of Attila's hordes—pointed helmets with rolled turbans round them; brass visors with slits for mouth and nose and eyes—visors of very terrifying aspect somehow; the wide, heavy-quilted gowns of the old Mongol Horse, that were known in Europe in the early ages as the Scourge of God; short, curved, steel bows and bristling quivers of arrows; little round shields and short, curved swords.

Thereafter, two attendant lamas come in with something hidden under a scarf, which presently is revealed, as they place it upon the prepared little painted plinth in the centre of the arena—the rough-made figure of a man, about a foot long, fashioned of dough, and painted. This serves as the double representation of Langdarma, of whom we have heard, and of anybody who has followed his evil footsteps—you or me, or the one in the crowd about us who feels the cap may fit.

It is a somewhat diminished "corpse" nowadays. I fear the influx of European visitors has rather spoilt the Ladakhis' pleasure, since no longer do we see the realistic and larger article, that was built up artistically with organs of fowls, and whose limbs duly bled forth good honest blood of goats, and from whose "little Mary" might be extracted eerie-looking coils of quite genuine "innards." I believe in the remote and dim ages they actually used to put real portions of deceased criminals into the "corpse," but that practice disappeared anyway in Ladakh long before any Europeans came on the scene.

Then enter the black hats again, in a ceremonial dance around the corpse, making mystic offerings of *chang* and barley-meal—a lengthy process—sprinkling the *chang* and flinging the grains of barley about the stage.

As they withdraw, the demons sweep down and the ghouls enter also—white, pallid figures, with skull-shaped masks, and long fingers and toes to their white garments, to give them a skeleton appearance—tight-fitting white garments, picked out in red, to represent the bones.

They dance fantastically round the corpse, dashing up to it, and threatening it with their ghost daggers, dashing away with wild shrieks, sweeping in again, and once more dashing out. Sometimes they are chased away by some saintly figure who performs charms and incantations, but presently they are back again, waving their daggers.

Then comes the great stag-headed, blue-faced, skull-crowned god of hell with his sword, and stands over the corpse. He waves his sword about it as though to carve it in pieces, yet somehow missing it each time, and perhaps he, in turn, is repelled for a space by the intervention of some benevolent figure.

But the end is certain—at last he will suddenly swoop down on the corpse and bury his sword in it, the ghouls will clamour round and carve it into little pieces, which they stuff into their cavernous, skeleton jaws. And here for some strange reason a lama stands beside the corpse. Whether the idea is to show that the lama is powerless to save the evildoer who has neglected him during earthly life I cannot say, but that is the impression it gives one.

Thereafter, from the tragic the scene turns to the grotesque. Enters an old teacher—a fat buffoon of a mask, who can barely walk—attended by a riotous train of impish schoolboys in pink masks. He installs himself on a seat, and proceeds to teach his flock, who mock him the whole while, and his ill-directed blows with the rod he holds fail always to reach the delinquents. I was told this figure represented the false teachers who, from time to time, have arisen in the history of Buddhism. The horseplay goes on for a long time, and draws shrieks of laughter from the crowds, most of all when one daring youth possesses himself of the rod and castigates his pantaloon of a master.

In the early part of the afternoon of the second day a very interesting ceremony takes place—the blessing of the animals. I think the idea is that of the scapegoat. When I saw the Hemis play, there were three lots of animals—two yaks, some ponies, and a couple of dogs.

They were brought into the courtyard clothed in rather gaudy *jhools*—the horses richly caparisoned. They were first censed—to which the yaks objected strongly, and they were formidable yaks, with three men apiece on the ropes to keep them from damaging the crowd or the officiating lamas. They were then sprinkled with holy water several times and, lastly, daubed with red paint.

Thereafter they were led three times through the monastery buildings, faster each time, until at the last entrance the ponies were doing a good canter, and the yaks, with lowered horns, chased after the men who held their nose-ropes, and, amid, the shouts and yells of the crowd, all disappeared in a mixed-up mass through the narrow entry passage. They are supposed to carry off the sins of the people during the past year and, I believe, in Greater Tibet—I have seen photographs of it—one of the yaks is actually slaughtered, and a low-caste man is appointed scapegoat, being adorned with the yaks' entrails, and driven into the wilderness, where he casts off his gruesome decorations, and with them the sins of the people, thereby earning a fee.

Then at last the show breaks up, the evening is devoted

to festivities of all sorts, and the play is over until next year.

You go back to your little camp with a very mixed impression of quaint masks—grotesque heads and terrifying ones; shrieking figures in rags, dancing skeletons, and dog-headed figures clothed in leopard-skins; old-time warriors and stately priests; mitred censer-bearers and ghoulish demons; great silk hangings and ragged nomad shepherds; priceless Chinese brocades and tattered garments; and with the scent of incense in your nostrils.

Later you will be visited by some of the lamas seeking reward for their part in the entertainment, bearing you joss-sticks of China, in exchange for which they hope to receive the coined silver of King George. The schoolboy novices of the burlesque are well to the fore in demanding baksheesh.

When they have gone you will be left in peace to dine, as darkness comes on, and be able to sit out in the moonlight again—well wrapped up against the cold, for the Hemis gorge is somewhat higher than the Indus Valley, and chilly after sunset—and listen to the strange music breaking out again, music rendered even stranger now from your impressions of all you have seen these last two days.

Then on the morrow, when you take the road back to Leh, among the throng of returning sightseers, you will come back to life as it is—to the sunlit glaring track, the white stones, the little green-fringed villages. But you will, I think, come back with some comprehension of the people who for years and years have insisted on talking about Mysterious Tibet, and included Ladakh in the term—quite incorrectly as regards the name Tibet but, nevertheless, not so incorrectly in their application of the word mysterious. There is, to my mind anyway, something of "mystery" attached to this strange little country set high among the high hills—something quite different from all the other parts of the world—some indefinable charm hanging about it—something which owes nothing to, and suffers no detraction from, the manifest tawdriness and gross superstition which leaps at once to the materialist Western eye if the mind behind the eye has not the gift of questioning further.

CHAPTER THIRTEEN

THE CENTRAL ASIAN TRADE ROUTE

CHAPTER THIRTEEN

The Central Asian Trade Route

WHEN people begin to talk of going up to Ladakh the first question you hear asked is "When do the passes open?" That probably sounds strange to folk at home, accustomed as they are to being able to go anywhere they like at practically any season of the year. But for travellers in this part of the world it is a very important question, because there are only certain seasons when you can travel at all—that is, if you are travelling in the usual way, with a convoy of animals.

Winter snow is the factor, and most of the passes are shut to animals and, as a rule, also to men in any numbers from December until April—to middle or late June in the case of the higher ones, although height is not the only factor. There are also direction and glaciers to take into account, so that sometimes you find higher passes, which are ice-free, and with a north and south aspect, open earlier than lower ones, which have bad glaciers, and face east and west.

During those months there is no possibility of getting animals over—laden or unladen—and on many of the passes even laden coolies cannot move; the only living beings who could cross would be a small party of lightly laden, stout-hearted men with a weather-wise leader prepared to take risks.

That is the difficulty of the Central Asian trade route, which runs between Yarkand in Chinese Turkestan, and Srinagar in Kashmir, nearly eight hundred miles over seven passes, of which three are really bad, and three are over 17,000 ft. high—the lowest crossing-places in the great mountain ranges they traverse.

The first of the three bad passes is the Zoji La, out of Kashmir, which, however, is only 11,500 ft. high, and owes its evil reputation to its extremely heavy snowfall; the other two are the Khardong La, leading from Leh into the Nubra district, and the Saser La, which takes you out of the Nubra Valley, over the Karakorum range, and down the upper waters of the Shyok river. Both are glacier passes, and their heights are 17,400 and 17,600 ft. respectively. The Saser is reputed by the traders to be the worst pass on the whole road, and, although I do not know the two Turkestan passes, I agree with them as regards the others. The Saser lies in a nest of eleven glaciers, surrounded on both sides by high peaks, which culminate six or seven miles to the north in K32, somewhat over 24,000 ft. high, and on the south in the Nubra trio of peaks, two of 24,000 ft. and one of 25,000 ft.

The Khardong La should be open in early June—

though it may be rather later some years—the Saser La should be passable by the end of that month, though it is often July before the caravans come over. The traders' chief object is to avoid the first forcing of the passes, and so you will find men kept in Leh to send word north if a caravan is leaving Leh, and men on the Shyok side of the Saser waiting to send news in of the approach of any party from the north. Eventually some extra stout-hearted soul does risk the first crossing, and then the caravans begin to move.

The opening of either of these passes may fairly be called mountaineering, and this year I had the good fortune to be with the Shaksgam Expedition when they forced the Khardong La on the 13th June.

From Leh to the pass itself is a matter of some twelve miles, the first nine of which lie up an ever-narrowing valley, enclosed by low, stony hills, a valley once glacier-filled, down whose centre lie the great stone blocks of the terminal moraine formed as the glacier retreated, for now there are no glaciers on the south side of the pass.

There is a certain sense of adventure when one is setting out to cross a bad pass for the first time in the year, and as your caravan marches out of Leh, under the little gate on the Khardong road—attended by half the friends you or your men have made in Leh, come to see you safely off—you cannot help a slight thrill as you turn your eyes from the fertile expanse of the fields about Leh—the clusters of buildings, the hill-perched towers and monasteries, the long lines of *chortens*—and look forward to the snow-clad hills sweeping up in front of you—dazzling white against the cloudless blue sky—and mark the long, white valley up which your road will have to be made over the still virgin snow.

You will perhaps be moving with ponies, although these will not be able to cross the pass laden, and will have to be changed for yaks at the evening halt. A better plan will be to have had the yaks brought down from the higher reaches, where they usually live, and loaded in Leh, for this will save you the change of load—an important factor if, as you must, you start to-morrow, up the last bit of the pass, at somewhere about half-past two in the morning, so as to get hard snow.

You rise steadily, mile after mile, until you have passed the last fields, and at an altitude of about 13,000 ft. turn into the valley leading up to the pass, making your way over frozen streams and snow-beds, in the shady corners, until at last you come out into a wider, flatter expanse at the snow-level, probably 15,000 ft. in the early part of June.

There you will find your camp being pitched for the night at the junction of the two streams which meet at the head of the valley, before the actual climb to the pass begins, while beyond you lies the somewhat steeper incline to the pass itself—an untrodden expanse of white snow, concealing a tumbled mass of boulders, which render the road so far more difficult if you wait until the snow gets soft.

It is cold here, for the sun disappears early behind the surrounding hills, and you will want all your warmest clothes, and be very glad of warm food and an early bed, though you may find considerable solace in the marvellous view as you look back to the long line of hills on the farther side of the Indus. You sit in the grey shadows, watching them catch the last evening light on their snow-capped summits—a great chain of flaming red and gold peaks, under a rapidly darkening sky, whose translucent cobalt is changing to indigo even as you watch it, while the peaks pass from rose to madder, madder to green, to blue, and then to cold white.

You may be able to force your way over next day, but in all probability you will have to spend the day in breaking trail up to the head of the pass, and down a little way on the farther side—driving your unladen yaks, who act as snow-ploughs—your men following with every spade or axe that you can muster, to improve the way.

And by the time you make the head of the pass and, clambering up the last steep little bit of snow, come out on the flat, narrow summit just as the sun rises, you will probably find that you have done about enough for that day, especially if it happens to be your first ascent that year. The air will be strangely thin and insufficient, and you will, in all probability, have collected a headache even if you are not one of the few unfortunate people to whom heights and Channel crossings are identical in the symptoms of internal disturbance they produce.

You will probably sit down thankfully and pant for a space before you stand up to admire the view ahead—peak after peak flaming into view, with, giant among them all, the great Nubra Peak, 25,000 ft.—the Chang-lung Gipfel of Hermann Schlagintweit—the first big peak of the Karakorum chain, rising above the still hidden Nubra Valley, whence will lie your road forward.

Then next morning, if your yak-men will face it, you will do it all over again, only this time the yaks will be laden and the unladen ponies, if you happen to be taking any over, as we were this year, will be following—fighting for breath as they plod over the snow—sinking in the soft places, and from time to time giving up the contest, for the pony soon loses heart in deep snow.

Your men will be manhandling them, and if you are wise you will have ropes handy, for they will be wanted on that last steep rise—a couple of ropes, and ten to a dozen men to haul the unladen ponies up to the crest, where they will stand with hanging heads and distended nostrils, every bit of energy gone for the present—dead-beat animals, with here and there cut legs bleeding on to

THE LAST HUNDRED YARDS ON THE KHARDONG PASS.

Getting a pony up to the top, at 17,400 feet, in June.

the white snow—cuts from the snow-buried rocks, where they have slipped—cuts from the glass-like edges of hard ice.

Some of the men, also, will be very nearly beat too, since in addition to hauling the ponies up the slopes at a height where even walking makes you pant, until you get acclimatized, they will have had to manhandle up loads taken from yaks or dzos who have plunged out of the trail and got sunk in drifts.

I always think that the sight of a caravan at the head of a high pass is a very fine picture of endeavour, one of the things that make you glad to be a man among men—to see your rough-clad drovers, wisps of yak hair tied over their eyes to prevent them going blind from the glare, panting slowly upwards with their loads. Here is a little group of half-a-dozen getting a tent-pole under a sunken animal's belly to heave it clear of a drift—there a dozen hauling on ropes to pull an animal free—a couple more, beat for the moment, gasping on a snow-buried rock, seeking enough breath to face the last hundred feet—and on the summit a knot of men resting for a space, breathing great deep breaths. And yet most of them will be laughing as soon as they have any breath to laugh with—after they have rubbed the life back into frozen fingers and toes.

All this, of course, is only on a fine day—in a snow-storm or a blizzard there is not much laughter, the business is too serious—literally a matter of life and death for many of the animals, and perhaps for some of the men. And there is nothing to see save the driving flakes. The last time I crossed the Saser La it snowed the whole day, and at times one could not see a dozen feet in front as one floundered along; long icicles hanging from beard and moustache; men and animals numb and stiff, with one only thought—somehow to keep on the trail, and so in time reach some place of shelter.

But on a fine day, when everyone is up on the pass—when the last animals and the last loads have reached the divide—then you feel fairly entitled to bask in the sun for a while, to cook a meal in the shelter of a rock—and thank the gods for the blessings of hot tea and tobacco before you start down over the snow again.

The north side of the Khardong La is the worse of the two, since the track—existent only in late summer—lies over a glacier. In the early summer it is easier if you start very early in the day, since your way lies over hard snow, which is not bad going—indeed you yourself may glissade if the spirit moves you, though your laden animals cannot. Reasonably hard snow is, to my mind, always preferable to ice, since the animals do not slip in the same way—however hard it may be, within limits, their feet grip, to a certain extent.

And so you plunge downwards for fifteen hundred feet or so, to pull up at the frozen lakes below the glaciers, and look back up at the long black line of men and animals treading their cautious way down towards you. Then on again over the snow, hour after hour, until at last you reach some patch of flat ground, bare of snow, where you can halt for the night and wait for your transport to struggle in—your last animals probably not arriving till well after dark.

You will not get up early next day, but will lie abed and be thankful that the pass is behind you; that, for the best part of the next hundred miles, going will be comparatively good, and that by this evening you will be well down below the snow. Later in the day you will make Khardong village, at a humble 13,000 ft.—really a summer resort only, since its inhabitants go down during the winter to camp along the Shyok Valley, or live in caves under the river-cliffs, leaving just a few men to look after the houses.

The day afterwards you will be down in the Shyok Valley, following the cliff-hung road, above the rapidly filling river, snaking your way across rotten conglomerate faces, with sheer drops down to the splintered rock at the edge of the stream, until in time you come to Khalsar, with its pleasant grass camping-ground, at the mouth of the silvery torrent pouring down the narrow ravine from the snow-beds and glacier behind.

There you can bask in the warmth of a modest 10,000 ft., and take inward pride at the thought of being the first party over the Khardong this year, for there is always good human elation to be felt whenever you have forced a pass. The road will be empty, of course, but you know that Leh bazaar will be humming to-day, and the people who have waited and gathered there during the winter will even now be making their way up to the Larsa, following in the trail you have broken, and that news is going forward up the Nubra and over the Saser that the Khardong has been opened, and that in ten days' time the Saser will probably be forced, and so the northern caravans can start coming down.

The Shyok Valley is far more impressive than that of the Indus, for the hills are much higher and nearer to you. You get a real sense of being walled-in here as you look up at the immense mountains of snow-capped limestone and granite that tower into the sky on either bank. It is desolate too—the villages are few and far between, and there are no fields in the river valley, only upon the glacial fans which you cross at intervals.

After leaving Khalsar you come in time to the Tirit suspension bridge, the only one over the Shyok—at least you used to come to it, it has just been washed away—an imposing modern structure of wire-rope and stone anchorages—altogether Western-looking, save only for the ragged old lady who guarded it, and for the prayer-flags she had tied on to the stays to keep off the wind- and water-devils. I crossed that bridge several times this year, and she always asked for baksheesh, which she was promised conditionally on the demons not carrying it off, a jest that tickled her old mind tremendously. She got that baksheesh only just in time, though, for the demons took it away for good and all in October, and I only hope they did not take the old lady as well. However, her little hut was built on a rock platform, a bit higher up, with a fine red anti-demon *hlato*, so perhaps she escaped.

Tirit is a tiny gem of a village set in a wider expanse of the Shyok Valley, rich with fruit-trees and crops, and in July with masses of dog-roses, which are the summer dress of the Nubra Valley, whose mouth lies half a march below Tirit. It is less shut in than the rest of the Nubra villages and gets the sun early and late, so that it makes a pleasant camping-place. Once the passes have opened, the road is thronged every day, and you may pass two or three caravans in a day's march, as from below Tirit you turn up into the fertile Nubra Valley, which is known as the Garden of Ladakh, though I think the person who so called it suffered from a combination of optimism and poetic fancy.

It is certainly fertile and, lying as it does somewhat lower than the Indus Valley, is rather warmer in summer. On the other hand, it is shut in, and so in winter gets bitterly cold, as the morning sun comes up so late. I know places in the Upper Nubra the late September sun does not reach until eleven o'clock, and is gone again at three, so that by December I imagine there is next to no sun at all, day after long dreary day.

But it does look green as you enter it, and in July and August it can be quite unpleasantly hot, marching over the heavy sand in the middle of the day, as you follow the trade route through Sumur and Tiritsha, and in time come to the last cluster of villages in Ladakh—Panamik and its adjoining hamlets. The greenness is largely due to the coarse jungle bushes, which fill so much of the river-bed, and enable the Nubra villagers to have thorn-fenced fields instead of the more usual stone-walled ones. There is a fair abundance of wood, too, and I can quite understand anyone coming into the Nubra from the northern side, after the bleak marches over the Depsang—the utter desolation of the Upper Shyok, and the dreary Thalambuti Gorge—getting a little poetical at his first sight of the fields and scattered apricot orchards of the Nubra Valley.

The Nubra river in summer is a fast-running, muddy torrent, quite impossible to cross, save only at Taksay, where they keep an antiquated Noah's Ark kind of boat, in which you can risk your life for a few annas. It is an exciting crossing, because the stream runs really fast, and although the actual crossing is under eighty yards you shoot downstream nearly two hundred yards before you make the opposite bank. It is quite enthralling to watch the shouting crew trying to hold her sodden timbers' nose on the current, and baling for dear life. And as you climb higher and higher on to your perch, in an endeavour to keep your legs dry from the in-pouring water, you can do some fine calculations as to whether the sinking-point will be reached before you make the shallow sandspit downstream on the farther bank, which the old man at the steering-paddle is apparently trying to aim for.

The people of the Nubra live, for the most part, on the caravans. Firstly, they are carriers, and gain large sums from that; and day after day during the summer you may watch the Nubra ponies setting out for the Saser La, with the little black dzos plodding along with their bundles of fodder for the ponies. There is no more fodder or supplies to be bought after Panamik, and it is something like eighteen days before the trade route reaches human habitations again, with very little grazing on the way, so that most caravans starting out have to carry a good deal of forage. The usual way to do it is to charter a number of Nubra animals to put you a week out on the road, after which you load what is still left of the fodder on to your own animals, and hope for the best.

In Panamik there is a big State granary for the traders, which is kept filled by the Nubra people paying their taxes in kind—an economical arrangement, that saves having to transport grain and fodder from the Indus districts.

Then, besides carrying, the Nubra people make a lot by selling sheep and fowls, eggs, milk and butter to the passing travellers, and they are probably a big factor in the abandonment of the Shyok road, which was partly constructed at big expense before the war. It leaves the Indus Valley by the Chang La—a glacier-free pass —and avoids the Khardong and Saser passes, the two worst on the road. But it involves a six-day march up the Shyok, through a country devoid of inhabitants and supplies. Nevertheless, I think it would be well worth keeping up in view of the number of animals' lives that would be saved, for the greatest loss takes place on the Saser Pass. Moreover, with fair luck, the Shyok route would be kept open practically the whole year, for the Chang La can be crossed in winter, whereas the Khardong and Saser are utterly impassable from January to the end of May, even in the best years.

You will probably stop at Sumur on your way to Panamik rather than at Tegur, which is the proper stage, because Sumur is rather a fascinating little village, with a big yellow-cap monastery, most ornately frescoed. It is the biggest *gompa* in this part of the world, and the Skushok, as I have already mentioned, is an artist of note. You will observe, too, that there is a change coming over the buildings as you work up towards Panamik; there is something more of Chinese influence in people and buildings alike, so that you find *chortens* with regular, upturned Chinese roofs, and villagers who, in garb and feature, seem quite different from those you first saw in the Indus Valley—fairer in colour and very Chinese in feature.

For this is the old trade route, not only of Central Asia but also of China, since time immemorial, and the caravans that come down now with Chinese tea are probably the same in almost every way as those that came in from China in the days when William of Normandy was getting his ships ready to sail for Pevensey, even as far back as the days when Julius Cæsar was conquering Gaul.

CHAPTER FOURTEEN

NUBRA & THE SASER PASS

CHAPTER FOURTEEN

Nubra & the Saser Pass

THE English explorer, Moorcroft, is the first European who has left any record of having visited the Nubra Valley, which he called "Nobra," naming the Nubra river, the "Charasa," from the village of that name, on the right bank. He made a short trip there in May and June of 1824, proceeding by way of the Digar Pass, one of his intentions being to pay a visit to the hot springs of Nubra, which are supposed to be valuable for many complaints, notably for rheumatism.

He mentions finding the springs at Chusan, the farthest point he reached. The springs are situated actually about a mile short of Panamik, and I do not know the name of Chusan. During the three months when I was camped in and around Panamik my two Pathan orderlies were full of praise for the waters of these springs, both for washing and drinking purposes. There are no signs of volcanic action anywhere, but the water where it comes out from the main source is too hot to put your hand into. Two rough bathhouses have been constructed, and the temperature lowered by leading in a spring of cold water. All around the ground is covered with soda deposits, and a few miles farther downstream is a wide expanse of tussocky grass-land where, during the winter, the soda oozes up, and is collected for sale, being much used, both as soap and for clarifying the butter-tea which the Tibetan drinks.

Moorcroft seems to have been impressed with "Nobra," which he described as "picturesque and pleasing." I think that he must have been somewhat easily pleased on this occasion, because the Nubra Valley is rather overrated. True, the villages are fertile, and the mass of trees and the plentiful flowers, wild roses and wild iris, are pleasant sights to the wanderer accustomed to the naked, savage hills; but, that apart, the Nubra Valley is as gaunt and stony as any of the other Ladakh valleys, while the villages are poorer-looking and, to my mind, not very picturesque.

But if you like to climb out of the great walls which enclose the valley you will see scenery grand enough to please even the most *blasé* mountaineer: mile after mile of snowfield and glacier, peak after giant ice-clothed peak, and, in the distance, the long wall of the Karakorum sweeping away to the north-east.

About twelve miles upstream from Panamik the trade route turns out of the valley up the narrow Thalambuti gorge, to climb its long, winding way up to the Saser glaciers, and then down again to the upper waters of the Shyok river, which, pouring down from the Remo glacier, flows first south-east and then, turning nearly due west, eventually picks up the waters of the Nubra, as it continues on its way to its junction with the Indus, in Baltistan.

The little patch of country near the divide, between the Shyok and Nubra rivers, from about ten miles short of the Saser Pass, is, to my taste, one of the most fascinating corners of mountain country that I know. It lies on the main Karakorum chain, and shows all the features associated with that giant among the world's mountain system. Having got as far as Panamik we might push on and have a look at this outer wall of Nubra, the beginning of the waste spaces that divide Ladakh from the Chinese "new dominion"—Sin Kiang or Kashgaria —*alias* Chinese Turkestan.

The trade route is now open, and as we march out of Panamik in the early morning we shall see many Yarkandi merchants and drovers, and every little garden and thorn enclosure will be filled with Yarkandi ponies, resting after their long, hungry journey, and picking up a little condition from the Nubra grazing before setting out on the last stage of their long journey and facing the labours of the Khardong Pass.

Panamik is very small, and made up of widely scattered houses, among terraced fields all carefully thorn-fenced, so that the hungry ponies of the trade route shall not strip the place bare of every bit of green.

It boasts no monastery, only a few rather ornate *chortens*, and a *chorten* gate such as one meets in many places, a gate surmounted by a *chorten*, and whose archway is generally adorned with fresco paintings. That of Panamik is filled with pictures of the amorous blue gentleman we met in the monasteries, only in Panamik he and his lady are depicted in every colour of the rainbow—here in blue and green, there in red and white, here, again, in grey and yellow. I used to wonder if the pictures were intended to cheer up incoming travellers after their three weeks' march, without seeing any other human beings save the passing caravans on the road.

We make our way over the fan of rushing waters pouring down from the big rock gorge on our right, whence lead the irrigation channels that support the valley, for, as elsewhere in Ladakh, the Nubra depends on melting ice, and all the narrow *lungpas* conceal great glaciers—the side arms of the great Siachen glacier, which once extended right down to the Shyok at Tirit, in fact at one period blocked that great river and turned it into a lake.

The gaunt rock hills spring straight up on either bank to a height that is nowhere much less than 5000 ft. above the 10,500 ft. where we stand, and they are only the beginning of the range. A mile or two behind them, again, glimpsed now and then for a moment

THE MAMOSTHONG GLACIER IN THE EASTERN KARAKORUM.

This is a view taken from the East Bank at a height of 18,000 feet

through rock clefts, rise greater hills—peak after peak of 21,000 ft. and over, up to the dominating ones of 24,000 and 25,000 ft.

Our way lies through two small hamlets, similar to Panamik, but even more scantily populated, and then, the last fields and trees left behind, we make our way over a long, dazzling expanse of white sand and stones, with every now and then the whiter remnants of the unfortunate ponies and donkeys who have been unable to struggle in those last half-dozen miles to the grain and fodder of Taksay or Panamik.

Midday should see us at the mouth of the Thalambuti, having first passed some gigantic rocks, splintered granite boulders bigger than the average Ladakhi house, where half a hillside came down and destroyed a project of fields and irrigation channels that were being made. The Nubra Pass never had the courage to begin again; evidently, indeed obviously, the demons objected to the birth of a new village, and so to-day Sasoma lies desolate, save only that you can trace here and there the remains of the water-channels and retaining walls, where the falling boulders have not entirely crushed them.

The actual entrance to Thalambuti gorge is impassable, for the water pours out through a knife-cut ravine, not more than twenty feet wide at bottom, the whole drainage of some fifteen or sixteen big glaciers and a score of smaller ones, with a catchment area of anything between 150 and 250 square miles, much of which is snow-covered even in summer, and all of it under snow in winter.

On the farther side of the racing torrent of grey water, spanned by a bridge of poplar trunks, guiltless of hand-rail, the road—a good, built-up pony-track here—winds its slow way up a rock face for a little over two thousand feet, in some sixteen or seventeen zigzags, some of them literally cut into the face of the steep, sloping rock.

Coming down it you may see a slow-moving caravan of laden ponies and donkeys, or a string of unladen dzos, who have returned from carrying forage over to Saser Brangsa and been unable to find an incoming caravan with load to be brought down.

It is a steep ascent and tiring for the animals, and we shall reach the top some time before our laden beasts and be able to rest at the little red *hlato*, the pyramid of stones and horns, with a prayer-flag or two, which the Ladakhi always erects at the summit of a pass, the highest point where the road begins to descend again. From the 13,000 ft. *hlato* we can look back and take our last view for the present of such things as trees and fields, houses and other signs of human life, seen far away at Ayi, on the opposite bank of the Nubra, which, from here, looks almost as though seen from a low-flying aeroplane.

In front of us the road drops very steeply to Umlung, where we shall camp to-night—a narrow space under the great cliffs, perhaps a hundred yards in length and fifty to sixty broad. It is made of stone, but the original lack of level surface has now been compensated for, and Umlung is comparatively flat, thanks to the few million animals which have halted there night after summer night for many years. The first time I passed through Umlung my Pathan orderly started digging out the accumulated dung to pitch my tent on clean ground, and I had to point out that he would be digging all night before he reached ground, so he might as well not worry.

But the accumulated manure gives fuel, and so long as the weather is fine and dry is not offensive. When it rains it is another story.

All the following day we shall climb and climb steadily, sometimes on cliff-hung tracks, sometimes over glacier moraines, very weary going, until late in the afternoon we come to the mouth of the big Mamosthong glacier, which name means the "thousand sheep," because the advance-guard of a Mongol invasion perished there, killed like sheep by avalanches. Ladakhi names are nearly always descriptively picturesque like that, and have a meaning of sorts, if you can find it out.

Here, at about 15,000 ft., we will camp for the night, either at Pangdongtsa or Skyangpoche, on comparatively open grass-land, where the animals can find a few mouthfuls of grazing, and there is a little *burtsa* shrub to be got for fuel—a smoky article, but preferable to the usual manure, in that it doesn't make your tea-water quite so pungently scented.

I spent a very fascinating month at Skyangpoche this September, exploring the hills and the glaciers around, and can recommend it to anyone who is interested in high mountains and glaciers, since they will have a fair three-to-one chance of being able to say that each new peak they set foot on is virgin snow or rock or ice. The Visser worked the south side—the glaciers mostly; Dr Arthur Neve and Oliver went up the Mamosthong glacier and climbed the col at its head, and I have scrambled about some of the glaciers and the lesser peaks both north and south. Otherwise, the Shyok Nubra divide is virgin ground and crammed with stately peaks of anything from 21,000 ft. upwards.

They are all nameless, of course, for there are no inhabitants, and the Ladakhis and Yarkandis who pass along the trade route go no higher than is absolutely necessary to cross the Saser Pass. So not only will you be, if you go off the trade route, the first European to set foot on peak or glacier; you will, in all probability, be the first man who has ever done so.

From Skyangpoche, over the Saser to Saser Brangsa, in the Upper Shyok, is a long and weary day's march in fine weather, and all days you are either winding round under glacier snouts or passing over great glaciers. Most of the halting-places do have names, as usual descriptive ones. One in particular I remember, at the very snout of the great glacier up which you pass to reach the saddle-shaped glaciers forming the actual Saser Pass. It is "Bong ro Chan," the "place of the dead donkeys." I do not know why they call it that, since the name would apply almost equally well to any point on the road between the Nubra and Shyok rivers. It may be, perhaps, that the road there is very narrow, only four or five feet wide between the rock wall on your left and the ice wall on your right, and, therefore, since you have to pick your steps among the skeletons between the boulders, they are more noticeable than elsewhere, where the vultures—who make a fat living—generally drag the carcasses a bit off the track, so as to feed undisturbed.

The Saser Pass must be one of the hardest bits of road in the world, and the queerest pass in constant use to be found anywhere, for it is made up of two big glaciers, which sweep in from the north and south walls of the valley, coalesce, and then flow east and west, one draining towards the Nubra and one towards the Shyok.

In the centre are several high-piled moraines, which serve more or less as guiding marks should heavy snow hide the trail of skeletons. It is impossible, of course, to make a road over the moving ice of a glacier, all that can be done is to send up parties of men each year when the snow has melted, somewhere in late July, say, and clear a track among the stones that will last for the rest of the year.

On a fine day, in brilliant sunshine, when the snow has mostly melted, the Saser is not too bad. The only difficulties are the altitude, to which by now you are probably acclimatized, and the slippery ice, where a laden animal can so easily fall. If you take the trouble to examine the scattered bones you will find countless shattered leg-bones, which show that the late owner slipped somewhere, and, weak and tired, came down in a heap on the hard ice and broke a back or front—usually back—leg.

The Yarkandi generally, I think, cuts the animal's throat forthwith, for he eats horseflesh in places like this. The Ladakhi is not so merciful, and I have several times regretted being unarmed in that locality, and made a resolution to carry a merciful pistol with me on future trips, should fortune let me go there again, for the Ladakhi does not always take the trouble to kill his useless beast, and it may lie there, in the bloodstained snow, watching the vultures collecting.

There is no doubt that the cold and hardships of high places tend to brutalize the lower type of man, and sometimes, in bad weather, when you meet a caravan, you can see the effect in the dull, heavy figures, muffled up on their overladen beasts plodding drearily through the blinding snow—ice-covered from head to foot—hardly opening their eyes and breathing no word to each other or to the passer-by.

In the late part of the year Leh Hospital is filled with cases of frost-bite—wretched, ill-clothed men with gangrenous hands and feet; perhaps, even, an unfortunate would-be suicide, who, from cold and misery, has tried with his frost-bitten hands to cut his own throat, and, as usual, cut it in the wrong place. It is a hard life on the Central Asian trade route if you happen to be a hired ponyman travelling with a callous Yarkandi merchant, of whom there are some to be met.

I remember, coming down from the Saser one day in a driving snowstorm, trying to force a woman back, for we knew she could not reach the pass before dark, let alone cross it, for she was already half-dead with cold, and her pony was starved and lame, as was also that of the sixteen-year-old son who accompanied her. There was a missionary with me who spoke Ladakhi, and we had a Ladakhi who spoke Turki, and we wrestled there with the couple in the driving snow, but nohow could we induce them to turn back. She said her husband was just in front—we had, indeed, seen him only a mile back on our way down, a fat, ugly man on a good horse, waiting, so he said, for his party. So we gave them what food we had, and with many misgivings let her go on, not that we could have stopped her anyway, since she was unwilling, and you cannot come between the Mussulman and his female possessions.

Two days later, however, going up that way again, I met a cheerful Indian merchant who had just come over, a loquacious and hospitable gentleman, who looked upon my orderly and me as brothers in a strange land; the more so when we talked of the Northern Punjab and the home which he had not seen for thirteen years. He told us that the ugly Yarkandi husband on the good pony had *not* waited; on the contrary, he had hurried over the pass to the comparative comfort of desolate Saser Brangsa, and that another party had picked up the woman's body after snow cleared the following day, and when they brought her down to Saser Brangsa the husband was already well out on his way to Murgo, beyond.

Such a fate would never have happened to a Ladakhi woman, nor, I think, to be honest, to any woman travelling with Indians.

The pilgrim women are to me rather a feature of the road, for they face the hardships every whit as courageously as the men—riding laden ponies in the same way, distinguishable in clothing only by the wisp of veil they sometimes tie around their features when they meet a European; they do not worry about the Ladakhi men, whom, I think, they look upon as merely animals.

I remember a couple whom I saw on the march several days on end, all their belongings on their two ponies;

On the Head of the Saser Pass in August.

On the March in the High Nomad Country. Yak transport at Chakas Talas, near the Pangkong Lake.

an elderly man with his middle-aged wife—and she shamed me badly by walking up the Thalambuti Pass hanging on to the tail of her laden beast, whereas I stuck to the saddle till the halt at the top. However, my pony carried nothing save me and my fox terrier, whereas hers carried an old tent, rolls of bedding and a month's food, so there was a slight difference.

They are plucky souls, and for them a pilgrimage to Mecca is no light undertaking, and I think they deserve the honour they get on the return to their own homes, for they have risked a great deal on their journey, and faced a road that is no light job, even for a fairly hard man.

The Saser Pass is disappointing, if you expect a view like you get from the Khardong La. It is rather shut in, and the nearer hills hide the real giants, while in front of you, towards the Shyok, there is little to be seen save what now seem to you lowish hills—rocky creatures of humble altitude, of nineteen and twenty thousand feet, not so very much higher than the ice-col, where you bask in the sunlight against a pile of stones, and make tea for the midday meal with a handful of dung or *burtsa* that you have brought with you.

Then on again down the eastern glacier, over a trail of ice-borne, loose rocks, mingled with white bones, until in time you slip off the side of the ice-stream just before its snout, and come back once more to solid ground, to drop steadily downwards until, at a little over 15,000 ft., you reach the desolation of Saser Brangsa. Here, among the smoke of cooking-fires, marking where the weary travellers are settling down for the night, there are the remains of a stone hut, and multitudinous pony and donkey skeletons, mingled sometimes with a few camel bones, for the Khirghiz bring their camels as far as this —the so-called Karakorum Pass in front being ice-free, though actually higher than the Saser.

Below you races the Shyok river, fresh fed from the Kumdan glaciers upstream, and from its parent, the great Remo ice-stream, hidden behind the jagged rock hills to northward. Before you a wall of hills, with long slopes of black and red detritus, a mass of rock pinnacles and boulders, mile after mile of stones and grit, and here and there a tuft or two of withered herbage.

As you sit there in the sunset, and look out over the valley, I think you can safely say that, although you have marched 350 miles to get here, never before have you seen anything so lifeless and void of beauty as this Upper Shyok Valley.

Across the river lies a narrow valley cleft in the hills, down which you may perhaps see a small party of men and animals splashing their way to the fords. It is the Murgo defile, through which the road continues, in country easier than that you have passed, but, if possible, almost more lifeless—the long road that will wind on and on over the Depsang plateaux and the Aghil ranges, until, in time, it drops down to the deserts and oases of Chinese Turkestan.

But from the point of view of inhabited country you have now left Ladakh a long way behind; there are no more villages or monasteries, no more *chortens* or *mane* walls; you have come into a no-man's land, where there are, literally, no men, no flocks or herds—no life at all, save only for the caravans of the summer and autumn, which plod their weary way from stage to stage, north-bound or south-bound, through water-swept defiles and over high passes—over boulders and sand and snow and ice. Yes, undoubtedly God made the mountains, and then made man to climb them—made the trackless wilds, and gave man the spirit and wit to make ways across them. You realize the truth of this at places like Saser, when you watch the caravans coming in, and perhaps you, like me, will be glad that motors and aeroplanes cannot come there—that there are still places left on the earth where man must fight Nature as Man, with only the aid of living animals, and not by the power of inanimate machines.

CHAPTER
FIFTEEN

TO THE PANGKONG LAKE

CHAPTER FIFTEEN

To the Pangkong Lake

AS I have already said, Ladakh lies athwart the main Central Asian trade route—that connecting China with India. It also has two lateral routes running into Tibet from Baltistan and the country westward—routes following the Indus and Shyok valleys respectively, and finally meeting near the Tibetan border. The importance of these routes is nothing like so great as that of the Central Asian one, but nevertheless there is a good deal of traffic on these roads, mostly that of caravans of wool and salt coming from the East, and of grain and dried fruit travelling eastward from Ladakh.

The Shyok route, from the mouth of the Nubra as far as the Khardong Lumpa, where one turns south towards the Khardong Pass, and so to Leh, follows the main Central Asian road. Thereafter, however, in summer it lies along an ill-kept hill-track, since the river-bed is flooded, and you have frequently to make your way up and down steep spurs, sometimes nearly a thousand feet from the water, over little *parris*—cliff-hung galleries of tree-trunks overlaid with more or less flat rocks—and then down again to the hot sand and boulders.

And nowhere in the long weary march from Khalsar to Aghiam will you pass a village, a house, or a field, and the sole signs of human life you see will be the two villages of Rongdu and Satti, on glacier fans, for across the racing grey waters of the Shyok, cut off for six summer months from the southern bank, it is even more lifeless than the Lower Shyok, and the hills that tower thousands of feet above you—naked rock hills—add to your sense of being shut in away from the world of men.

You may perhaps pass a small caravan of laden sheep from Rupshu—big animals compared with the sheep of Ladakh—each carrying a little pair of rough-woven bags, full of salt or soda, going down to Baltistan. Or, perhaps, you may meet a few diminutive laden dzos on the road. Ponies you will not often see, for the summer road is thought too bad for them, with its precipitous drops and *parris*, and the dzo is considered safer, as being more sure-footed, owing to his yak ancestry, and as less temperamental and less likely to sudden fright. The Shyok summer road is no place for a pony to shy. The winter road is better, since it follows the sandy river-bed, and at times lies across the frozen river itself.

You leave the Shyok at Aghiam, which the maps mark as a village, and which does actually possess three houses and several fields, as well as a good deal of thorn-jungle. In fact, as you debouch from those last weary miles of wind-tossed sand, Aghiam strikes you as a particularly green and fertile spot, unless, maybe, you strike it when there is a summer sandstorm blowing, and you can barely see ten yards ahead of you.

From Aghiam you follow a track leading up the *nullah* under conglomerate cliffs, that have a nasty habit of sending down loose boulders on the heads of the unwary, mile after mile of bush-clothed torrent bank, where on your right foams down the water from the Diger Pass—an alternative way back to Leh, out of the Shyok Valley, which is easier than the Khardong, but involves two extra marches for those trying to reach the main Nubra trade route.

Then suddenly you swing northward again round a projecting cliff, whose foot is garnished with many rather decrepit *chortens*, and so find yourself in sight of Tyar, at a height of some 13,000 ft.—a little village of the hills—long rows of terraced fields, a cluster of mud and stone huts, and soft mud and conglomerate cliffs springing sheer from the valley, crowned by a quaint little monastery.

Tyar is the first village on the western side of the Nobok La, the pass which leads from the Nubra and Shyok areas into the Chang Tang country, and your Ladakhis will tell you that you are now going into the *Chang-pa*, the nomad-country, as they call it, although for four days' march yet you will still find villages and see buildings and fields.

Tyar is a typical village of the passes, and you meet small herds of yaks the same as at Khardong and Khalsar and other such villages over Ladakh whose inhabitants' chief business is the conveying of merchants or travellers over a pass where most of the year yaks are essential.

Next day, having exchanged your little dzos of the Shyok for big upstanding yaks, you set out again, still following the valley uphill, over rather a difficult road —difficult even as Ladakh counts roads—and after a ten-mile march, which takes you till the afternoon, you arrive at the *larsa*, under the Nobok La, at an altitude of about 15,500 ft.

A *larsa* is one of the commonest features of North and East Ladakh, indeed, of most parts of the country. It is a flat place, comparatively speaking, preferably one giving a certain amount of grazing when the snow has melted off, and it may, perhaps, be embellished with one or two rough stone shelters, guiltless of roofs. It is what its name implies—the foot of a pass—the place where you spend the night before tackling the pass itself, or where you wearily fling yourself down after you have made your way over the divide, and wait for the animals to come in.

The Nobok Larsa, on the Tyar side, is somewhat more attractive than most, since it is rather more open, possesses a fair amount of rich, lush turf and many wild flowers, and is ringed round with low snow-covered hills and glaciers of very Alpine aspect—nice tame glaciers and mountains, nothing like so wild and forbidding-looking as those in the Karakorum.

Nevertheless the Nobok La has its terrors also. The first time I crossed the Nobok one of the yak-men taken on at Tyar was carrying my big camera. He was a finely built, youthful man, very cheerful and ready to laugh, and in his Mongol way good-looking. It was only when I suddenly turned to him for my camera to take a photo that I noticed that he fumbled rather, and kept his hands hidden in his long sleeves, which are to the Tibetan and the Ladakhi, and to most peoples of the hills to north and north-west of India, what gloves are to us. And then I saw that his hands ceased at the knuckles in unsightly knobs of pink and white, and thought I had to do with a leper. Only the man looked so robust and healthy that I doubted, and made inquiries. He had been benighted on the Nobok the previous year, and, though his feet had escaped, he had entirely lost all his fingers and both his thumbs from his night in the snow. Once again I wondered of what stuff the Ladakhi is made that he could still laugh, and be really cheerful, mutilated as he was in that cruel fashion.

However, in summer the Nobok La, despite what some people have written about it, is an easy pass of 17,000 ft., ice-free and practically snow-free by August. Even in July there were only three or four hundred yards of snow to be crossed, just at the last steep slope under the pass itself. But it was a bad pass from the point of view of its effect on the party, with the exception of myself. Everyone else was ill, which was absurd, since by then they had all crossed many higher and more difficult passes. The finale was when Vagrant, my fox terrier, took the disease. I have never seen a dog look so utterly haunted with the fright of a strange *malaise* that he had never met before. He dodged round from rock to rock, dashed and hid under my knees, bolted back to get comfort from my orderly—who was in no great case himself—and, finally, tried to hide. In the end I had to doctor him with brandy, which restored him far more quickly than the others, and we set out again—all very much the worse for wear.

"Pass sickness," as the Ladakhis call it, is a strange and incomprehensible thing, since you cannot foretell it. Height alone is no criterion—nor is cold—nor is wind. One Ladakhi theory puts it down to the poisonous scent of certain purple flowers—I think a species of primula—which commonly grow on the upper slopes of passes, and, if they can, they avoid going near the flowers. Certainly the Nobok La was crammed with them, so that the theory may have something in it. Moreover, I have noticed that my men were more often upset on a pass than when climbing hills considerably higher than the passes, and the wild flowers are more commonly found in the passes than on the naked rock hills to either side.

From the Nobok La a long and very dreary march takes you down to Drugub—too big a distance to cover in one day really, but you can do it if, as we happened to be on that occasion, you are in a hurry to get forward.

The valley is quite one of the most dreary places I know—devoid of life or habitation—an old glacier moraine of immense boulders which, at far later date, has been cut across by the stream of still extant lateral glaciers and turned into a chaotic wilderness of stones and watercourses through which you pass. I took a photograph of it once, the usual disappointing type of photograph which shows what appears to be a close-up bit of a beach of the foreshore at home. Only when you put a magnifying-glass over it do you realize what it really is, as some smaller black pebbles among the bigger white ones resolve themselves into big laden yaks, with little men walking alongside.

Drugub is the junction of the Chang La route from the Shyok to the Indus Valley—a long, level expanse of fields and a certain number of rather poorly built houses, for the country is now visibly poorer than that which we left even on the other side of the Nobok La, and you begin to agree with your men in the differentiation they make between the *Chang-pas* and the inhabitants of the lower districts of Ladakh. The people are even more raggedly clothed; ornaments are fewer and very tawdry, and the women no longer worry as to whether their garments fasten over well across their ample bosoms.

The first time I passed through Drugub it was a great occasion, for on the other side of the stream I observed a black-clothed Leh merchant just moving off with his ponies, and on inquiry found that he had spent a week there, selling his goods and gathering up the Drugub people's earnings of the past year. That must be a great event in life—the annual visit of a "shop"—for, naturally, there are no such things as shops in either the Nubra districts or in the Chang Tang country. But every spring some of the Leh *banias* and shopkeepers go out with a string of ponies laden with luxuries, such as tea, a little sugar perhaps, tinsel trinkets, bags of grain and bales of cheap cloth, and sell them to the local people in exchange for skins and wool, and salt and soda.

Think how much nicer England would be if, every May, Mr Selfridge and Mr Pope and Mr Bradley loaded a few pack-animals and marched out into the wild districts of Brighton and Eastbourne, of Ashford and the forests of the Weald, or risked their lives among the nomads of the Cornish and Welsh borders! Think of the gatherings round their tents and the hurrying throng of women, fearing lest all the farthing looking-glasses should have been sold out, or the coral beads come to an end.

I think there is a great deal to be said for a life like that, and I am sure it must be much more amusing to set out on the road with your pack-animals and bales than to sit at a large desk (I know all commercial magnates have large desks, which never have anything on them but a telephone and an ash-tray, because I have recently been looking through the catalogues of a famous firm who undertake to furnish your office), for you see pictures of commercial magnates looking at a large map and planning "campaigns," a term I used to associate solely with my own prehistoric, brutal and licentious profession of soldiering, until I discovered that the world's real campaigns are really planned by forceful-looking men who hold certificates from Schools of Salesmenship. No one really knows how the world is governed until he reads the advertisement pages of our modern English magazines, and the ornate ones that come to us from the other side of the Atlantic.

I suppose the Leh shopkeepers also plan their campaigns, in their little booths in Leh bazaar during the winter, even if they have no maps, desks or telephones, but, anyway, they come out over the passes and wander about for weeks in the villages and among the nomad encampment, and return with bulky loads of fleece and fine *pashmina*, which must represent profits to the tune of many hundred per cent. on their original outlay.

To my mind Tankse is really the beginning of the nomad country, the next stage in front of Drugub, a fascinating place, with a lot of fields and very few houses. But above the willow-garden where one camps rises a long, steep, hog-backed hill in the centre of the valley, covered with buildings, and walled wherever the natural slope of the rock is not steep enough to prevent anyone climbing it. It is old Tankse, which the Dogras sacked in 1841, at the end of the last abortive rebellion, and since then no one has ever lived there and the houses lie empty, and the old palace at the summit is empty also. The sole inhabitant is a wizened old lama, who attends the one-room chapel on the hill, small and dark and smoke-begrimed and very old, which he told me had been miraculously protected from the Dogras. I expect they overlooked it, for it is a bit out of the way, in a dark corner, and, anyhow, there is nothing very rich to steal—a few paintings, a few brass lamps, a plaster image or two and one old book, whose stained cover is embellished with ancient brass buttons of forgotten Indian regiments.

A moonlight night at Tankse gives one, I think, one of the most fascinatingly eerie landscapes that could be wished for. The long ridge on which old Tankse stands looks, in the moonlight, like some prehistoric giant animal, with slate-grey hide, rising up the valley, and around are lesser creatures, with great heads and spiny backs, by daylight merely outcrops of rock and tumbled moraines, mute evidences of the Ice Age that once was here, but in the magic of the moonlight converted into monsters waiting to spring out from the shadows upon the lonely wanderer.

From Tankse you have a choice of two roads into the nomad plateaux—the northerly one, which lies along the shore of the Pangkong Lake, and the southerly one, known as the Nomad road—both of which meet sixty miles away at Shushal, which is, so to speak, the metropolis of nomadland, and owns several little houses and two real monasteries furnished with a lama and a half, the half being about eight years old and rather shy.

Let us take the northern road to the lake on our way out along the wide, turf-grown valley, sloping gently upwards from Tankse 13,000 ft. — a good grazing-ground for numerous ponies and yaks—where you will meet Tibetans of Rudok with their animals, swarthy men, bigger than the average Ladakhi, bareheaded and loud-voiced and of loud laughter—an independent-looking people.

We may perhaps also meet a real Tibetan lama on his way in from Lhassa to the big yellow monastery of Sumur in the Nubra, which has a close connexion with the home of the Dalai Lama. A lama of Lhassa in his travelling clothes is somewhat different to the loose-gowned, high-capped people you see in the Ladakhi monasteries, for on a journey the yellow cap will be replaced by a close-fitting fur cap with long side-flaps lined with lamb's-wool, and on his back will be a pack like that carried by the Baltis—an affair of twisted willow branches, in which will be all his worldly possessions, the whole topped by a sacred book or two. He will hurry by you with rather a hunted look, for he is unaccustomed to Europeans, and not a little frightened, since he knows—he has heard—that you very often carry little black boxes which, if pointed at a man, by some strange power take part of his soul away in visible form, and perhaps if you are evilly disposed this may be burned, or have pins stuck in it, or made to wither up, and then the man himself will follow suit.

Climbing imperceptibly but steadily, evening will see us encamped at Chakar Talao, by two glacier-fed lakes, under gigantic cliffs of white marble, where there are no trees, no brushwood—nothing to burn save yak-dung, if we can find it. Chakar Talao is wildly beautiful at sunset, with the high mountain walls on either side—walls of white and red marble above the yellow-green of the sparse herbage, where the big yaks wander, picking up such grazing as may be found. With the moon above the cliffs, after the sun is hidden, it looks still more beautiful in its unearthly fashion as the wind sighs over the rippled surface of the silvered water in the now swollen lakes, new filled from the melting ice after the heat of the afternoon, and which to-morrow will have sunk again to the day-level before the sun gets warm enough to fill the torrents that pour down from the cliff-hidden glaciers.

Then in the early dawn on again, still working upwards over stony expanses of river-bed, snouts of moraines filled with blocks of purest white marble, until we reach a little red-painted *hlato*, which marks the end of our two days' ascent, and, turning the corner, see before us a great sheet of peacock-blue under low rounded hills, in whose hollow shoulder project the sharp ends of glaciers—the Pangkong Lake, some fifty miles long, with a breadth varying from five to eight miles—a slightly saline lake of translucently clear water, the remains of the great sheet of water formed long ago by the score and more of glaciers that used to sweep into it from either side.

It looks like an arm of the tropic sea more than a lake, with its wondrous colours of blue and green—the greens and blues of the peacock's tail—the colours that one sees in the water around Aden, and the hills beyond are somewhat the same, but softer and more rounded—hills bare of tree or shrub, nothing but mile after mile of gaunt bare rock, and yet filled with soft colours borrowed from the sunlight in the way that only naked rock and sand can do.

As we follow it hour after hour along the sandy track, running only a few yards from the water's edge, hour after long sunlit hour for the best part of two days, it will seem more than ever like the sea—sometimes like parts of the Mediterranean—where, farther on, we follow corniced tracks under high rock cliffs. Only here are no flourishing fashionable towns; only twice shall we pass the tiniest of hamlets of three and four houses apiece, and once, at nightfall, the bigger village of Mang, several miles of rough grass-land dotted with the tents and yaks of the nomads, and with a few scattered houses and a rough *mane* wall or two.

Here we shall be closer to the glaciers, which hang low above us, for we are now higher and on the north side of the hills, where the snow lingers later and the glaciers continue century after century for all that they are dwarfed now and no longer reach the plain about the lake, where, however, their tracks lie clear to see as we wind our way past the tumbled moraines, marking where the ice-streams once flowed.

It is a different country now—almost flat for long miles together, surrounded by low rolling hills, up most of which you could ride a pony. Gone are the gaunt pinnacles of the Nubra, gone the knife-cut gorges of the Shyok, gone the steep hog's-back *arêtes*, flecked with bars of snow and divided by long glaciers and ice-falls. This is an easier country for all that the valley bottoms are higher and colder, as the rough fields and the few stunted crops tell you. It is high plateau country—the fringe of Greater Tibet—of the flatter uplands of nomads and flocks and herds instead of the terraced Alpine villages and fertile fields we left in the Indus and Shyok areas.

And when, after another long day's march from Mang, we turn south-east from the great lake, pull over a long ascent and look down on Shushal, with miles and miles of grassy plateaux round it, we shall agree with the Ladakhis that we have indeed come into a country which is not Ladakh at all though, politically, it forms part of it. The last few miles over swampy grass-land into the little willow plantation of Shushal, with its solitary monastery, is something quite different from all the many stretches of road we have traversed since we left Arcadia, something altogether other and yet in its own way as fascinating as were the bleak gorges, the high snow passes and the scorching expanses of sand and old moraine, which are the main features of the Ladakh river valleys.

CHAPTER
SIXTEEN

THE ROAD HOME

CHAPTER SIXTEEN

The Road Home

SHUSHAL lies in truly nomad country, and although it boasts a few buildings it is in reality nothing more than the winter headquarters of the nomad shepherds and herdsmen, whose flocks of sheep and goats and yaks can be seen wandering over the wide plains.

Most of the nomads live in tents, which are not unlike those used by the Afghan *powindahs*, who come down to the frontier districts of India each winter, returning with the approach of the heat to their cool upland grazing-grounds in Afghanistan. The tents are woven of black yak-hair—a coarse fabric—low wide tents with a long hole in the roof, supported on a couple of poles held by many very long ropes, the longest of which are anchored out at a distance nearly three times the length of the tent itself, kept taut by forked branches cut from poplar- and willow-trees.

All around during the daytime will be piled the coarse bags for carrying fodder or yak-dung fuel, the wooden pack-saddles for the yaks, and playing about will be a swarm of children, unspeakably ragged and dirty, but cheerful. The nomad peoples seem to have more children than do the villagers of the more settled parts.

There are dogs too, a-many—great rough-coated animals, much sought after as watch-dogs, and usually when you meet a party going down from Ladakh you will find one or two Chang Tang puppies led behind, or, perhaps, if very young, carried by a coolie in a basket, for they are in great demand in Kashmir as watch-dogs. They sell for what in Nomadland are high prices—as much as five or six rupees for a good sealed pup, for the puppies are sealed on their foreheads with a great blob of sealing-wax by the owner who has bred them, and the quaint Chinese seal is to the nomad fancier what a pedigree is to us. They are very strong puppies and grow into enormous dogs, but savage and of uncertain temper, so that when you approach a nomad encampment the first thing you see is a rush of the children to precipitate themselves upon the big dogs, on which they literally sit until you have departed again.

They are of valuable possession to the Chang Tang folk to guard their flocks against the depredations of wolves and leopards, and also on the edge of Tibet against brigands and other masterless men. But they are difficult to domesticate, in our sense of the term, and dislike being in a house, which is something of which they have no experience and no racial memories, so that those you find in Leh for instance, where people keep them as watch-dogs, are nearly always tied up outside, even at night.

The Chang Tang country is the main resort of the big-game hunter from India, its easier hills and grass-filled valleys offering cover to large numbers of the big wild sheep and goats whose heads adorn so many messes in India. Every summer there will be a score or more of energetic souls who march up for their two or three months' leave in the hope of securing some of the coveted trophies—a very much better way of spending a holiday than the new fashion, which one saw appear after the war, of "poodle-faking" in hill stations.

The Ladakhi who, as I have mentioned, does not hunt or fish does not understand the *sahib's* habit of undergoing considerable discomfort and undertaking a lot of strenuous climbing and marching in order to shoot animals with large horns, wherein he differs from my following of Pathans and Kashmiris, who found it difficult to comprehend a lunatic like myself, who, instead of spending his time in the proper pursuit of the Oriental gentleman of leisure—viz. killing things—marched hundreds of miles and climbed thousands of feet merely to produce "pictures" (the word for photograph or map is identical). I am afraid I tried their patience rather high sometimes in the matter.

But some Ladakhis have a solution of the problem, which a talkative Ladakhi dame gave away to us once. Among the various anti-demon devices which fill Ladakh you have already noticed the *hlatos* of yaks' horns and engraved yaks' skulls. Elsewhere you will also find those *hlatos* made up of the horns of wild game, and among these are sometimes to be seen the kind of horns of which the sportsman dreams but which he rarely, if ever, sees.

Obviously to the Ladakhi mind we also must be seeking heads for the same purpose, although we shoot the owners, whereas the Ladakhi picks up those of dead animals. Yes, the lady knew quite well why the *sahib-log* came there. They came to get the big horns, which they preserved and took away, and then mounted them on pieces of wood and hung them in their temples to pray to. She knew this because one of her husbands had once been down to Kashmir and India and seen the horns being got ready, and had, moreover, gone into a "temple" and seen them there.

This is a perfectly true story, for all that it recalls the part in *Kim* where they find the regiment whose officers every evening worship the statue of a bull with mystic rites. And such an idea would seem far more natural and understandable to the East, which is always very seriously concerned with religion, than would the idea that you put up the heads merely as trophies, endeavouring always to bring back to your mess a bigger head than anyone else's.

From Shushal the nomad road to Tankse leads back across a comparatively high pass, somewhat over 17,000 ft., but exceptionally easy—two long days' march down a slowly descending valley, which for the main part is grassland, with a wide sluggish river flowing through it—rich grazing for the herds of yaks. From end to end there is no such thing as a house, but there are two recognized camping-grounds, where in the summer you will find the black nomad tents. The first rejoices in the name of "*kungma*," which merely means "upper," and the second in that of "*yokma*"—"lower." There is no other name, but they are descriptive enough, the first being about 16,000 ft., the second somewhat below 15,000 ft.

It is fifty miles with next to nothing to see as you march along the wide valley, under the low round snow-capped hills, with here and there a glacier or two showing up sharp-cut among the rounded snow slopes.

Then suddenly you begin to drop down steeply, and come to outlying houses—a monastery or two—*mane* walls, and so reach the outskirts of the cluster of villages extending eastward from Tankse—a very populous little stretch, in which I think the original inhabitants of Tankse must have sought refuge in the Dogra invasion and there remained ever since. For all that the fields lie at an altitude of close on 14,000 ft. they are very fertile in summer—thick crops of waving barley, watered by the little irrigation channels.

Nevertheless, as you follow the winding gorge into which the valley has now contracted, the slow-flowing river having changed to a true torrent, with here and there loud roaring falls, and presently come in sight of Tankse again, you realize that it is still the nomad country, that it is not the settled village life of Ladakh, and that these people would really be more at home in tents than in their tiny houses.

Across the river you still see the yaks grazing, and near the little bridge is a big caravan of sheep just off-laden, their little bags of salt piled up like a wall of stones and the bareheaded, pigtailed, felt-booted men squatting round the fire making their tea. It is still a nomad picture, a last glimpse of the roving country you are leaving, though you can see the beginning of the transition which has taken place all over the world, and is still taking place—the change from the nomad life to that of the settled farmer, and from him to the men of cities. And perhaps you will feel a little regret at the inevitability of the change, a little sorrow that it is the men of the cities who are the heirs to the future—that in a few more centuries the nomad will have gone—will have joined the mammoth, the giant deer, and all the other strange wild creatures whom civilization has hunted off the face of the earth.

And so from Tankse you will take the road back to Drugüb again, and then over the Chang La back into the land where people live on fields and in houses, and crowd together into villages and towns such as Leh, to which you will presently come back, and ride into the crowded market-places to see spread out all the wonders of the civilized world—little cards of buttons and packets of pins, oil lanterns, gaudy-wrapped packets of cheap dye, sugar and tea, and fearsome and wondrous cigarettes, packets of matches and cheap cotton cloths of India and Europe. Meet, moreover, a postman—in Ladakhi mufti, it is true—but nevertheless a postman bearing letters, and see another Ladakhi girt with the regulation leather belt and pouch of the Indian Telegraph Department. Meet also a white woman in a skirt instead of the breeches of the road; see a missionary in a store suit and a stiff collar.

You will even find newspapers—many days old, it is true, but still newspapers—which will be able to tell you what was happening in Europe only ten or eleven days ago, and give you all the latest "slogans" invented by the world's leaders since you left even comparative civilization—was it months ago, or was it really the years that it seems?

And perhaps like me you will wonder for a passing minute whether all those "slogans" and all the progress they claim to achieve are really quite so important as one thinks they sound in the middle of a crowd —whether there is not something a little better really to be got in the wild places, where money is hardly known and time means nothing at all. As you fall asleep on your first night in Leh, after looking out to the great hills and perhaps watching the moonlight come up over the snows and silvering the great dome of Mount Sacrifice, you may perhaps wonder a little about it all, and regret that in a few days your feet will be set to the long road which will lead you back in time to motor-cars, railways, newspapers damp from the press; yes, even in time to loud-speakers, both mechanical and human; to strikes and committees and "avenues" and all such things.

And you will wake with your question still unsolved, your musings unanswered—conscious only of one thing, that the curse of Martha is sealed upon your forehead, like the seal of the Chang Tang puppies, and that you must go back to be not even a machine—only a small cog in a tiny wheel of a gigantic machine instead of being a man.

I think when the day comes and you ride out of Leh again down the long dusty track to Spitok you will look back with not a little of regret, and with a great deal of longing, for all that you are leaving behind you, and perhaps feel at your heart the faint hope that someday the gods may be kind and let you return once more.

And then day after day as you ride along the road that takes you out of Lamaland, and see, in retrospect, all the places you have visited, and come at last to the border where you saw your first *chortens* and your first *manes* at the top of the long descent down to Kargil, you will know better than ever before how very much modern life contrives to miss, in spite of all the frills that it has added to existence.

But as you come over the Zoji, and look down again on the pine and fir forest and the flower-gemmed meadows, you will feel something of compensation—feel that you are being given something rather beautiful to sweeten the distasteful future—the wondrous charms of garden countries, which you will think you have never before known how to appreciate, as you can now do after months of the wilder, more savage parts of the world.

Even so, in spite of the fleshpots of civilization—the luxury of houses and clean table-linen, of silver and china and glass—the myriad "conveniences" of life as we know it—conveniences which some people will insist on calling necessities—you will look back also at the tree-clothed hills, behind which, far away, is hidden the pass that brought you back—you will look backwards, still with some faint feeling of regret.

At least if you do not do so, then obviously I have no excuse for producing this book, for it will mean that I have failed entirely to convey some tiny portion of the charm that hangs over one of the most attractive of little-trodden countries—of the quaint magic of Ladakh, which is Lamaland, and of the haunting call of the wild roads and the high hills.

INDEX

T

Map for "Magic Ladakh."

Seeley, Service & Co., Ltd.